Also by JOHN GRAVES

Myself and Strangers: A Memoir of Apprenticeship (2004)

A John Graves Reader (1996)

Hard Scrabble (1974)

Goodbye to a River (1960)

From a
Limestone Ledge

John Graves
FROM A
LIMESTONE
LEDGE

*Some Essays and Other Ruminations
about Country Life in Texas*

Foreword by Bill Wittliff

Illustrations by Glenn Wolff

University of Texas Press
Austin

Publication of this work was made possible in part by support from the J. E. Smothers, Sr., Memorial Foundation and the National Endowment for the Humanities.

First University of Texas Press edition, 2016

Requests for permission to reproduce material from this work should be sent to:
Permissions
University of Texas Press
P.O. Box 7819
Austin, TX 78713-7819
http://utpress.utexas.edu/index.php/rp-form

Most of this book has been previously published in *Texas Monthly*.

♾ The paper used in this book meets the minimum requirements of ANSI/NISO Z39.48-1992 (R1997) (Permanence of Paper).

The Library of Congress catalogued a previous edition of this book as follows:

Graves, John, 1920–2013
    From a limestone ledge : some essays and other ruminations about country life in Texas / John Graves ; new foreword by Bill Wittliff ; illustrations by Glenn Wolff.
        p. cm.
    1. Graves, John, 1920–2013—Homes and haunts—Texas. 2. Authors, American—Homes and haunts—Texas 3. Authors, American—20th century—Biography. 4. Texas—Social life and customs. 5. Country life—Texas.
    I. Title.

PS3557.R2867Z466 2004
813'54—dc22   2004045376

978-1-4773-0936-0 (pbk.)

This one belongs to Jane for many reasons, not least because without her I might never have stopped in one place long enough to recognize the profundity of such archetypal metaphors as chickens and fences and chewing tobacco.

Nor holds the world a better thing,
Though one should search it round,
Than thus to live one's own sole king,
Upon one's own sole ground.

Wilfrid Scawen Blunt,
"The Old Squire"

Then ask not wherefore, here, alone,
Conversing as I may,
I sit upon this old gray stone,
And dream my time away.

William Wordsworth,
"Expostulation and Reply"

Contents

PONDERINGS, PEOPLE, AND
OTHER ODDMENTS

Foreword

The first time Sally and I and the kids went to Hard Scrabble I had to ask directions from a thorny old gentleman sitting out in front of his house on the side of the farm-to-market road. "John Graves. Yeah, that's that fella writes those books." I said it was. "Hell," he said, "if I was to write a book, wouldn't be a marriage left in Somervell County."

A mile or so later we turned left onto a dirt road as directed, drove through a low water creek, then past a neighbor's pig yard where grunting mud-caked hogs lounged in old pock-marked porcelain bathtubs and urinals half-buried in the dirt. We opened and closed the Hard Scrabble gate, then drove on down the road a little way to a small rock house and a barn, both built by John. There was a canvas-covered canoe turned upside down on the barn rafters (not the canoe from the journey that became *Goodbye to a River*; that one had been given to a friend years before and wrecked in some mishap).

At the end of the barn was a little room where John wrote on an old upright typewriter, usually smoking or chewing tobacco. And of course there were books on the shelves and a long row of neatly labeled notebooks wherein John kept his farm records and notes on various—and mostly country— interests: cows and fences and honeybees and grapes and the like. Eventually these notes would be expanded into a number of articles written for *Texas Monthly* and later gathered and reworked for this book.

Outside, below the house, was a garden and an apiary and a compost so ripe you could warm your hands by it. There was a woodpile out back where one day I happened to find one of the two paddles John had used on his *Goodbye* trip. A cow had stepped on it, broken it in several places, and John had simply tossed it away, a tool no longer useful. (It's back in one piece now, and in the Graves archive at the Southwestern Writers Collection at Texas State University in San Marcos.)

And of course there were the animals: Blue the dog, Doorbell the Nubian nanny goat and her big brown randy billy goat son William, the ponies Lady Bird and Penny, chickens, Spanish goats, and a small herd of cattle.

There was White Bluff Creek where the Graves girls Helen and Sally would take our son Reid and daughter Allison to skip rocks and wade—and where Helen and Sally now take their own children on visits from homes far away.

All in all Hard Scrabble was—and is—what local country folk might admiringly call "a good place."

In the evenings we'd have supper out on the screen porch,

then talk for hours, long after Jane and Sally had sent the kids off to bed. (I teased John for oversleeping after one such evening. "Well, damn women, anyway," John said. "Keep you up all night talking, then don't get you up in the morning.") If it happened to be a Saturday night and the wind was blowing just right, we might hear ghostly whiffs of fiddle music coming from the little dance hall the neighbor with the pig yard had built out in his pasture just for the pleasure of his extended family. And if we stayed up long enough—and we usually did—we'd sometimes hear the foxhunters running their hounds through the creek bottom and blowing on their cow horn bugles just as their kin had done down through the generations before them.

The Graveses always had several projects going and usually within an hour or two of arrival we'd just naturally get folded into them. On one trip we kibitzed as Jane designed Christmas china for Neiman Marcus; another trip she was designing playing cards and candles. One weekend John and I repaired a water gap that had washed out during a flood. Another weekend we slaughtered a goat to make sausage, then made a mess of it with too much salt. This was somewhat corrected—but not entirely—by remixing it with several pounds of pork. On one trip John sent me up a tree to cut off a limb on which one of his hives had clustered after swarming. I did as instructed, and John, down below, caught the swarm in a cardboard box. Over the years there've been many trips, many projects; I can't go out there without thinking of what old Mister Charlie Goodnight said of the pull of his own varied pursuits: "I'll be damned if I could ever find time to lie in the shade...."

Hard Scrabble and John. It's where for more than thirty years now I've gone for good conversation, for inspiration, for friendship—and in times of crisis for advice. It's where I go when I need to be reminded that life—and the principles by which one lives that life—matter and matter hugely. This is not something John preaches. John doesn't preach. You just sort of get it by osmosis.

I'm not alone in this. Several generations of writers—and readers—have been drawn to John and his books for the same nourishments.

It would be impossible, I think, to overestimate John's continuing influence on his fellow writers. He has been the master for half a century now. His writing is the mark by which the rest of us scribblers measure our own.

Every culture, it seems to me, gets a handful of writers each generation or so who have the talent and ability to reach beneath the surface of things into those deeper currents that run through us all as fellow members of the human tribe. That is why great writing can be universal—why all great art in any field can be universal. It touches the commonality in all of us. It links us one to another. It links one generation to the next and to the next and to the next. It can link one man's experience of a river or a patch of land to all rivers and all patches of land in the world. That's what John did in *Goodbye to a River* and in *Hard Scrabble* and what he does in this collection.

The ability to write with such reach is a rare gift, but having the gift doesn't mean the work comes without effort. The gift of great talent may get you in the boat and put you out on the water, but you've still got to row the sonofabitch yourself.

No one knows this better than John—and no writer I know works harder at building his own symphony of words and thoughts and feelings to express himself than does John.

And another thing. I've never known John to publish anything large or small that didn't come up to his own standards of quality writing and thought.

There's something else about John. I'm not sure what it is,

but you just feel better after reading his books or being around him. You feel somehow enriched, enlarged, renewed....

You feel—and for me this is exactly the right word—you feel blessed.

BILL WITTLIFF

2004

Preface

These pieces all first appeared in *Texas Monthly* magazine in the same or similar form, but often under titles different from the ones used here. Some in a sense are footnotes to my book *Hard Scrabble: Observations on a Patch of Land*, in that they are expansions or variations on themes found there, though none is just a rehash and I hope all stand on their own feet. Others are concerned with more or less country things which came to interest me, or simply happened, after that book was finished.

Land, a whole region or just a piece of one, can be worn out in a relative, agricultural sense by abuse, as this little hill zone where I live and function was worn out a long time before I ever saw it, in the days of too much cotton and too many cows. It can wear a man out too, or wear him down badly, if he gets seized by the notion of restoring it to use and starts on that project perhaps a bit late in his life, though there's always a question as to whether the project or the years themselves are to blame. In large part *Hard Scrabble* is about such an effort, whose results as of this writing are not what anyone would call spectacular.

But a piece of land doesn't seem to wear your interest out and it doesn't wear out as a fount of comprehension and a way of living, not if you've really cared about it. Land and what people have done to it and what it's done to them aren't things you can understand fully, but you come a little closer with time, and you know more than ever that they matter greatly. So do weather and climate and stone and soil and wild creatures and plants, and so, for that matter, do livestock and farming, even if you run a two-bit sort of operation and administer it, as I do mine these years, with interested but easygoing (read sloppy, most of the time) benevolence, having learned by now that you aren't going to get everything done with your project that you once thought you might, and furthermore having no intention of letting it work you ragged in your remaining years. Let there now be contemplation, you tell yourself, contemplation and some placid enjoyment, even if the damned place is still not in shape.

I've believed for a long time that despite about two decades spent in fighting and loving a quite sorry piece of land, I could if and when I wished take one last walk over its rough surface examining what I have and haven't done with it, then could sell it and move away toward a different life without running the risk of turning to salt by looking back. Free will being a necessary illusion for some of us, I still believe this. I don't know that I'll actually do it, though, unless driven off by some extraneous force like heart trouble, bankruptcy, or the friendly neighborhood nuclear plant that is abuilding toward completion not very far away. One impediment to departure might be that vigor and time to shape a new life right aren't what they used to be (does this say something about free will, floating elusive somewhere between driven youth and cramped old age?), but chiefly my doubt has to do with the fact that I still haven't lost interest in the country and this piece of it where I live. Sloppily or not, there is still much to learn and watch and do, and for that matter enjoy.

In focus these ruminations are most of them regional, and at times even local. Provincialism shading into parochialism, some might say. Maybe. I hope I've got some small grasp of overall principles relating to rural land everywhere and the events that take place on it, but if I do I derived it principally from looking at individual spots in specific places, especially in this part of the world and on this battered stock farm, and I'd rather retail it thus. Unportentously, insofar as possible . . .

When writing the things that are here, I suppose I had in mind mainly city readers, which most readers of course now are. I grew up in a city myself, have spent time good or bad in a number of others, and have never wanted to pretend to a born rusticity that I don't possess. Native or convert countrymen will find some things to disagree with in these pages, or anyhow to cavil at. That is as it should be.

John Graves
1980

Coping

Notes of an Uncertain
Bluecollar Man

"The hell with it," said the seventeenth-century specialist. "I
spent nine years working on a Ph.D. and fifteen making full
professor, and here I am shoveling rocks out of a ditch. I'm
moving back to town."

"You don't mean it," I said, visitant free labor, leaning on
the pick that had loosened the rocks of which he spoke.

He managed a grin. "I guess maybe not. But one of these
times I will."

No figures exist nor is there much demand for them, but I
suspect that electrical malfunctions, leaky roofs, busted pipes,
jammed sewers, rampaging storm waters and the like have
more bearing on the number of back-to-the-landers who

3

eventually return to the cities than do other strong factors like wifely lonesomeness and the generally dismal economics, these days, of a functional existence on the land. Not that city-dwellers and suburbanites don't have to face similar troubles in their brick-veneer strongholds. But they don't have to face them quite so squarely and quite so miserably alone unless they choose to, nor is the possible range of problems half as extensive in town as out here among the hoot owls and the coyotes.

Consider if you will the question of human waste, to designate it by one of the numerous euphemisms which have been tailored for it and which attest to its grubby importance. Except for anal-stage babies and certain happy coprophiles and a billion or so Third World subsistence farmers, not many people have much affection for the stuff, but it is one of the more central facts of life.

A scant century ago if that much (let's not stray into debates over probably mythical Thomas Crapper and his invention and all that), Western man devised a means of whisking this substance out of sight and mind so fast that for most of us most of the time these days it is possible to pretend that it doesn't exist except as a source of metaphor. Whether this evasion is good for us philosophically is an unresolved question. Whether it's good for our world is all too easily resolved on the nay side, as a boat trip down any stream that has to absorb even standardly "treated" mass wastes will show. But that's a social problem, not a personal one unless you happen to live too close to the bank of such a stream or like to go on boat trips all the time. The average urban or suburban householder can keep his mind on higher things like bass lures and Archie Bunker except on rare occasions when T. Crapper's invention backfires or tree roots clog the short house sewer that connects him to the public main. And on those occasions he can call a nearby plumber, whose charges are

4

theoretically kept within reason by competition from hordes of other nearby plumbers, and with spouse, offspring, and intact dignity can quit the house till the trouble has been fixed and the air has cleared.

Not so in the boondocks. Here flows no public sewer main, but instead an intricate disposal system, consisting usually of a septic tank or two whose population of friendly bacteria digests solids (a second euphemism, though it includes other matter that gets flushed too), and a "field" of tile or perforated plastic pipe to disperse into the soil the clear effluent that results. Indigestible sludge results also, building up slowly in the bottom of the tank. This system isn't often a social problem but belongs to the sturdy homesteader alone. It costs large heaps of money to install and if he neglects it, letting sludge accumulate to the point that it spills over and clogs his disposal field, it costs heaps more to get it back into service. Hence a returner to the land, after one or two sour experiences, is likely to spend a portion of his time digging down to inspection boxes to lift their lids and make certain his effluent is unclouded, or searching about for damp fragrant spots in grass that hasn't been rained on in weeks.

And after a couple of other sour experiences with the payment demanded and received by one of the scarce and uncompetitive plumbers willing to drive out from a town and view his trouble and maybe cope with it, he is likely to spend a good bit more time manipulating a pick and shovel and certain more specialized implements such as snakes and sewer rods. Spouse and offspring may leave the premises with dignity at such times and usually do, but not he. Few of us neorustics, or paleo-rustics either, have the fortitude to tackle a sludge-packed septic tank on our own; we call in a professional with a tank truck and a large-bore suction pump, who gets revenge for the general unpleasantness and lack of social cachet attaching to his job by charging hell out of us. But most of the rest of it we learn how to do, because we have to.

So too do we learn about water systems that begin at the bottom of a two-hundred-foot well and progress through pumps and pressure tanks to an underground network of leak-prone pipes running to farflung cattle troughs and kitchen sinks and what-all, with swarms of differently sized and functioning valves and outlets along the way. And about high lines, ground rods, breaker boxes, and shorted motors. And diversion ditches, and chimney flashings, and one-lung gasoline engines, and termites, and even such mechanisms as water heaters and automatic washers, though with some of these latter you do have the laborious alternative of detaching the offending object from its moorings, wrestling it aboard your pickup, and hauling it to some city shop that will not stick you more for repairs than it sticks insouciant townsmen. In the course of this education you acquire a half-ton or so of parts and fittings just in case you need them, and boxes and shelves and walls full of tools, a good many of which you never heard of before you headed countryward and some few of which you will use exactly one time in your life— because for instance on one sole occasion you had urgent need of a one-and-a-quarter-inch crow's-foot wrench and nowhere to borrow one.

All for the dubious privilege of leading a technological life in a place where it possibly doesn't belong. And all aside from other technological maintenance and ingenuity with which your pursuit of agriculture, if any, may embroil you . . .

The only true alternative would seem to be a return to the simple forthright ways of old, which for that matter are still pretty much the ways of most of mankind. Privies and water-buckets, mules and muscles, handcarts and firewood and oil lamps or candles. Most of us who go to the country from a city background have some nostalgia for those ways, even if it only manifests itself in a wagonwheel hung over the gate

and an expensive fieldstone fireplace and a deluxe edition of *Walden* on the coffee table. And a certain number of us believe on principle that the old ways were more honorable in basic terms, since they fed on local renewable resources and individual effort and didn't gnaw at the earth's guts and disrupt the complex rich flow of its processes. (Not, of course, that some old ways of farming and grazing and hunting meat haven't been hugely disrupting the scheme of things since away back in prehistory.)

Yet, except for very pure and young and vigorous homesteaders of the Mother Earth persuasion, may God bless them one and all, the old-way alternative is a very tough one. Rewiring a barn and unstopping a sewer and sweating joints in copper pipe are small potatoes, in terms of effort and above all of expended time, when compared to the endless hauling and pounding and scrubbing and lifting and digging and chopping that characterized the daily lives of most of our rural ancestors unless they were landlords with serfs and peasants to command, or else the hardhanded fathers of large families. Or Henry David Thoreau, who had only his own basic needs to look after and could dine with friends in Concord when he felt like it, as according to recent report he rather often did.

We have tasted the fruit of the tree and found it sweet, and technology seems to be with us, even if there's room for a little hope that in time it may grow less destructive. Few women, having grown used to a Maytag, are willingly going to boil dirty clothes in a washpot or carry them to a creek and flog them clean on stones. And while there must be folks who consider a January outhouse, where the north wind whistles cozily about one's private parts, preferable to a heated bathroom, I haven't spoken with any of them lately.

Hence, stuck, one copes or one goes back to town. Most of us end up coping, most of the time, and paying through the nose for help when we can't. And most of us also end up

9

taking a perverse pride in the acquisition of such bluecollar skills, since it represents survival in a way of life we have picked. In the company of others eaten by the same disease, be they academics, Baptist preachers, businessmen, hairy dropouts, or actual born countrymen, we can always find a bridge for conversation in such topics as PVC drainage systems, tick invasions, and the merits of jet versus submersible pumps, and can brag to a discerning audience, impatient to start bragging themselves, about times when we have tracked down and rectified esoteric troubles. The high point of my own career in this respect came one winter day after an ice storm, when turning on the electric range mysteriously caused various lights in the house to come on and flicker dimly. By deduction and much snapping of switches and breakers and an uneasy rejection of my wife's theory of poltergeists, I traced this phenomenon to a meter-pole split-bolt connector, loosened by the ice's weight and jiggling in the wind, that was intermittently letting the juice from one of the range's hot wires flow out through the—well, never mind. It was a trifling sort of triumph, but it was mine alone.

You can go for months without much trouble and then have ten different sorts of it in a week, all urgent. I won't pretend that under such assaults pride doesn't often succumb to weariness and anger, especially as the years pile up on your back. You're supposed to be whatever it is that you are, in my case a writer, and you find that you've ended up a part-time, unpaid, and often unthanked jack of all manual pursuits. It is possible at such moments of realization, like my professor friend, to consider quitting or to yearn back illiberally and quite vainly toward a class society that would furnish you with a smart peasant or two or three to do such work and allow you, in the established manner of patricians and intellectuals, to take pride not in grubby bluecollar skills but in soft hands and happy ignorance of how things function.

Not that such wishfulness does much good when eleven heifers are bawling their thirsty heads off at an empty water-trough and finding and patching the cause of its emptiness is up to you and nobody else. And not that it usually lasts long. You go ahead and cope because you chose to be where you are and still like being there, and the coping is part of the bargain. And in it, too, you attain sometimes the pleasant illusion, rare these days, of dominating the world around you, technology and all.

More Than Most People
Probably Want to Know
About Fences

In his pleasantly irascible and intricately inquiring *Adventures with a Texas Naturalist*, the late Roy Bedichek lodged a complaint against the *Encyclopaedia Britannica* for its skimpy and lackadaisical treatment of the subject of fences, noting that the article on fencing—i.e., swordplay—is given about nine times as much space. I haven't checked the august *EB*'s latest edition, but for the vintage one I own the notation is accurate, and as a student of fences over a period of years I share Bedichek's resentment of this virtual dismissal of a major rural topic. I don't share his opinion as to its cause, however. In line with the testy sort of prairie populism that in his own way he embodied, he attributed the slight to aristocratic bias—"catering to the quality"—whereas to me the prejudice exhibited, if any, looks not so much upperclass as urban and academic.

For the fact is that most of the quality during history have derived their main sustenance and reason for being from the ownership and administration of rural land, and therefore fences have loomed as large and worrisome for them as they have for peasants and yeomen and whatever you want to call the rest of us bucolic sojourners. In two-thirds of our own sweet realm of Texas, for instance, if you went around looking for something that resembled a native aristocracy, the closest you would come would be the hereditary owners of large ranches, who are paid the compliment of imitation by many of our newly rich. No one on earth is more fanatically obsessed with fences than a rancher, nor do I think that the Old World descendants, spiritual and literal, of medieval lords of the manor and eighteenth-century squires can lag very far behind in their concern.

The big problem that fences cope with—or are supposed to—is of course most domesticated animals' flat distaste for staying where you want them to be. True, some fences are erected to keep people in or out of certain premises, but they are fairly useless for this purpose unless backed by armed might, as East Berlin wall guards could tell you, or any small-rancher in deer-hunting country. Owned beasts require some degree of management—for their own good, for the protection of planted crops and other things, for the maintenance of peaceable relations with neighbors—and in such management the ultimate tool is the fence, be it structured of wire, wood, stone, or living thorny things.

Not that it is the only tool. Under primitive conditions a main country occupation has been and still is that of the herder, guiding his charges through their daily perambulations and fending off Mother Nature's waiting teeth and claws. You can still see lots of them in places like Mexico and North Africa, where conducting forty-two goats about the rocks and brush is rightly considered a better job than none at all. But in richer lands like ours where hour-wage cash has become the major gleam on the collective eyeball, to afford such methods in their purity these days you need to be either a very rich and romantic yearner back toward simpler times when cowpokes and longhorns thundered about the open range, or else the owner of large numbers of vulnerable creatures under special circumstances, such as the immense migratory flocks of sheep that graze Western public lands under the sage eyes of imported Spanish-Basque *pastores*.

Lingering traces of fenceless times do show up here and there among lesser Americans, some of them quite interesting. Here in my own region only a few years back, a family of unmarried brothers of the sort known locally as "big old boys," though none was under forty, inhabited and operated a few hundred acres of ancestral land which was mainly rocky hills. Fond of hounds and hunting and fishing and hooch, they shared an aversion, not uncommon, toward the more or less endless maintenance that venerable fences like theirs require. Such effort as they occasionally expended in that direction went into restapling and sometimes splicing and halfheartedly restretching the three rust-rotten heirloom barbed wires that guarded those parts of their place's perimeter where neighbors had not built something better. Cross fences within the place itself they ignored.

Since they did some farming in creekbottom fields near the house and also ran about three times too many motley and ravenous part-Brahman cattle on their hills, this neglect could have proved troublesome, but they made up an ingenious game to counterbalance it. Though all were good riders and ropers, they seldom used these skills except when working calves. What they did was set up a sort of sentry post on the front porch, which commanded a view of the fields. During the growing season one of them would usually be sitting there with a full-choke twelve gauge and a supply of shells beside him, and when some intrepid bovine nosed too close to the rows of growing corn or milo, he would select a cartridge—number eight birdshot for close range, bigger stuff for farther out—and would loose a well-aimed blast.

It was a kind of training process, and it worked pretty well, give or take a few perforated ears and eyes among the trainees. A neighbor of theirs told me one February that he had lately gone down to inspect his lush oat patch, which lay against the brothers' lower boundary. "I've got a good net fence there," he said, "but I looked over at it and I seen a place where a big old deer or something had knocked the steeples loose and it was laying down on the ground. And just about the time I seen that hole, here come one of them boys' old bony Brimmers and she seen it too. But then she noticed there was green stuff on the other side, and she throwed up her tail and turned around and run like hell back where she had done come from."

However, most of us who have saddled ourselves with the ownership of land and livestock have less poetic imaginations than that, along with maybe less time for sitting on a porch with a gun. We need fences, good ones, or at any rate as good ones as we can afford in terms of money and/or personal effort, for this matter of quality in fences is very relative. At one extreme there is perhaps those brothers' three sagging brown wires. At the other is the solidity and permanence of masonry, and I doubt a stockman exists who would not like to have his place surrounded and crisscrossed with thick high stone walls if this were feasible, as indeed it used to be for patrician landowners in undemocratic times and places, where the fences they ordered built are often still upright.

A couple of years ago a young friend of mine made a forty-mile horseback trip with some *vaqueros* in an unmodernized part of Mexico, where all the big ranches were fenced with ancient five-foot walls of stones laid "dry"—without mortar, a difficult art, since strength depends on the mason's skill at bedding the rocks against each other and utilizing cumulative weight to bind them into place. There were hardly any gates, and when the party in its crosscountry, crow's-flight course came to such a barrier, the *vaqueros* would dismount and carefully make a gap in the wall, removing stone after stone, would pass through with their horses, and then as carefully would build it back again before proceeding. Such bred-in craft and patience with rock work are common south of the Rio Bravo and show up here, to many a yard-proud Texas country lady's delight, in quite a few of the amiable wetbacks who labor these days in our landscape.

But there is little likelihood that even very rich hobby-style farmers and ranchers are going to be able to fence much more than their yards with stone in times like ours, wetback labor or no. A hundred and thirty years ago, long before barbed wire, German immigrants in the Hill Country of south-central Texas were proud of their new farms and heartily disliked the open-range system that let other people's kine wander upon them at will. So they often built rock fences, doing it themselves if they were poor and had big families to help, or if more prosperous, hiring it done. The going price was four hundred dollars a mile, in an era when daily wages for hard long labor ran to a dollar or considerably less. I don't believe I'd want to examine a translation of those costs into the terms of today. Just the stone, if you had to buy it at prevailing prices in bulk, could run you eight or ten dollars per linear yard of fence.

Like stone, other traditional forms of fencing are esthetically pleasant, especially to the eyes of city folks recently enamored of land. However, they cost a lot themselves, and have some other drawbacks. A board fence around a horse paddock or a little mowed house pasture can be a handsome thing, but rot and warpage begin their work not long after the last nail is hammered home, as do the contrary beasts the fence is intended to confine and shield, who knock planks loose or splinter them with regularity either because there is greener herbage on the other side or simply for the hell of it. Not to mention all the repainting required . . . Similar problems afflict picturesque rail fences, whether of the zigzag worm type favored by our ancestors to protect their patches of cropland, or the fancier straight-line post-and-rail sort. I believe the prettiest of these latter I ever saw was in the fox-hunting piedmont country just east of the Blue Ridge, where non-Virginian money and taste have combined to preserve a reasonable facsimile of the eighteenth-century Old Dominion landscape, if you ignore a bit of pavement and a few Ferraris and such. It consisted of two feet of masterfully dry-laid stone in which were embedded the upright posts, with two split-chestnut rails strung between each pair of them and neatly mortised into holes. But the main reason it controlled the nervous highbred hunters in the pasture it enclosed was a single electric-fence wire fastened inconspicuously to insulators along the inner side of the top rail.

As for the Old World institution of hedges, the prickly impenetrable linear thickets, beloved of birds and other small beings, that outline many fields in the British Isles and Normandy and thereabouts, it never really caught hold on this side of the ocean, maybe because in eastern America in the old days there was a glut of wood for rails, and when settlers reached the prairies and plains where wood was scarce they had a rough time finding any thorny plants well enough adapted there to form a hedgerow. Before barbed wire showed up to meet their need they did try hard along these lines.

Here and there in central and near West Texas, as well as in states to the north, you can find isolated broken lines of spined bois d'arc trees which document that forlorn effort to cope with new conditions, and I believe the sometimes lovely wild rose that has turned into an aggressive pest along our coast was brought in for the same reason. Some Mexicans have skill at training prickly pear and cholla and other cacti into a fence around a small piece of ground, but I haven't met any Anglos who can do it—maybe, again, because it entails a lot of patience.

Perhaps we can omit consideration here of such expensive oddments as city-style chainlink fence, or those ingenious brick-lined haha ditches dug out in vanished centuries by very low-priced or chattel labor in mother England and parts of our tidewater Southeast (Robert E. Lee's birthplace at Stratford on the Potomac has a good example, as I recall), or flights of fancy like the fence someone had built a few years ago in my neighborhood out of upright pipes with oilwell sucker rods welded across them. That one held up well except where drunks had veered off the road and whacked it with their cars, and was handsome enough if you had a taste for aluminum-painted sucker rods, but sad to say it wouldn't hold calves. Some good working corrals are built that way, but higher and stouter and with more closely spaced rods.

And so we come down to wire, or "warr" as it is known throughout much of the state of Texas. Readers of Walter Prescott Webb's *The Great Plains* will recall that the barbed form of this commodity ranked right up there with the six-shooter and the windmill as an indispensable tool in the settlement of the Plains. It did away with the open-range system of grazing and the way of life that went with it, in the process causing rough armed conflicts here and there—warr wars, maybe a punster could call them. It allowed the introduction and proliferation of improved breeds of cattle, and along with a number of kinds of net wire is still as indispensable as it ever was, on the Plains and elsewhere too.

Many people dislike barbed wire intensely. It is of course mean stuff, designed specifically to inflict pain and thus to be repellent, and no one who has ventured afield and had its prongs rip his breeches or his hide or both, let alone worked bloodily with it in building or patching fences, is likely to waste much soft affection on it. Furthermore it has associations with violence and oppression, being linked quite correctly in the public mind with concentration camps and the ghastly trench warfare of World War I.

Most country-dwellers get past this revulsion because they have to, as a sewage-plant worker has to get used to the smell. But some continue to resist—most notable among them, I believe, being the owners of highstrung horses, and these have a valid point. Nervous horses don't mix well with anything on which they can hurt themselves, because if they can they usually will. We are much cursed, in these cedar hills where I live, with tangles of old rusty barbed wire that are the remnants of ancient fences dating back in some cases to the last century. Sometimes they have been balled up into real *chevaux-de-frise* by bulldozers clearing brush, and sometimes they are just lying on the ground where they dropped from rotted posts, waiting to snag your boot or pants cuff as you pass. Barbed-wire collectors, a special breed, think these archaeological remainders are fine, but nobody else does that I know of. Even if for years you have made a practice of throwing any pieces you see into the back of the pickup for hauling to the dump, some will still be waiting around. When a cow blunders into such a tangle she stops dead and carefully disengages whatever foot or feet have been grabbed, and goes her placid way. But a horse, especially a "good" one and especially with a rider on him, may well go into a frenzy, enmeshing all four legs before he's through and possibly severing some arteries and tendons. And he's capable also of tearing himself all to hell on a perfectly normal, upstanding wire fence.

There are some other objectors, too. I've noticed that the gentler sort of recent returners to the land, especially the younger ones, are wont sometimes to equate barbed wire with things like police brutality and military ways of thinking, a viewpoint that pops through occasionally in the publications they favor, such as *The Mother Earth News* and *Countryside*. Some are vegetarians of the purest sort and like their elder patron saints, Scott and Helen Nearing of Maine, eschew any form of ownership or exploitation of fellow creatures, which I guess eliminates worry about fences unless in terms of a neighbor's livestock. But more, probably, keep milk cows or goats, and pigs, and maybe some calm horses or donkeys for pleasure and work, and among these I seem to discern, as the movement advances in years and its adherents tend more and more to be tough survivors, a little less inclination to inveigh against J. F. Glidden's thorned and repellent invention.* The trouble is, it works.

The possible forms in which various kinds of wire can be combined to make a fence are myriad, and though to us country types the subject is fascinating enough to merit book-length treatment, I doubt the average reader would stand still for such a disquisition. The common form for cows, as practically everyone knows, is four or five evenly spaced barbed wires held up by wooden or steel posts to a height of four feet or more. Barbed wire can be made to serve for smaller stock as well if you want to go to the trouble of putting up eight or nine strands and making frequent inspections for the rest of your life to locate spots where staples have popped out or

---

* In case anybody wonders, as some wire fiend will, whether I intend to slither thus gracelessly past the uproar over who *really* invented the stuff, Glidden or Haish or someone else, the answer is an echoing yes.

wires have sagged, for hogs and goats in particular make a steady effort to find such places before you do and to get out, or in if in is where you don't want them.

Hence the utility of net wire, which can be in pretty sad shape and still keep serving as a reasonable barrier to such inveterate questers. It comes in a confusing array of sizes and shapes which I have no desire to enumerate. As an example, though, probably the most common net in my part of the country—at least since our Angora goat era came (and went, with the decline of the mohair market)—is what the dealers call 10-35-12-14. Decoded, this means it has ten horizontal line wires, is thirty-five inches high, has its vertical or "stay" wires spaced twelve inches apart (a requisite with horned goats, since the often-seen six-inch spacing causes them to get their damned heads harpooned into apertures, in which position they remain until defunct, or until found and arduously freed), and is composed of fourteen-gauge galvanized wire, twelve being better but more costly. It comes in three-hundred-and-thirty-foot rolls (twenty rods) and is usually put up in combination with three close-spaced strands of barbed wire above it to bring fence height to four feet and to keep larger stock from crowding down the net, as they will if given a chance since it has no prongs to prick them. And if hogs are around, yours or a neighbor's, you'll do well to stretch another barbed wire at ground level to keep them from rooting under.

Such fencing, given ordinary maintenance, will hold most domestic beasts usually found in our part of the world, though if you run mainly Brahman cattle, which are fine jumpers when hungry or panicked or randy, you probably ought to make it five feet high, and if like some you own exotic game animals or just want to keep your deer on the place and un-wanted hunters out, you'll have to go to eight or ten. Not that some hunters of the more endearing sort won't climb over any-how, or cut a hole for entry . . . But in my experience the worst enemies of net fences are horned bulls, a pair of which can utterly mangle a section of it when standing on opposite sides and bragging about how rugged they are. One stage of this game, after the early badmouthing is over, involves raking the head and horns back and forth across the stay wires, destroying them, and a frequent aftermath is that one bull suddenly finds himself where he has claimed he dearly wishes to be, on the other side with his foe, whereupon he may well flee in terror. Such displays of machismo are not usually visited on barbed wire, for obvious reasons.

Bulls aside, all wire is pretty strong stuff, but the effectiveness of that strength in a fence depends on how well you build the fence, for the best of wire is not much good if put up droopy and loose. It has to be stretched across the posts and has to stay stretched afterward so that the whole fence is a taut and elastic thing. The stretching is done with various tools and techniques whose description I will spare the reader, but it can only be done right if you have built adequate corner- and end-post assemblies to stand rock-firm against the pull of the wires that are anchored to them and of occasional beastly shoving. Among obsessed fence-builders, who are many, this is a subject of intense concern, as is shown by the numbers of enormous cedar trunks or sections of powerline pole that you see serving as corners in the countryside, some of them set four or five feet deep. For the less obsessed hole-diggers among us three and a half feet is usually enough, and a collision with buried ledge rock on a hot day can make us settle for even less.

Enough? All right, I won't go into the matter of different kinds of line posts and tamping and all that. Or into watergaps that are needed where fences encounter streams. Or wax lyrical about such items as the heavy-gauge net made up especially for the King Ranch and available to plain mortals too if they want to pay the tab, or the fabulous Ellwood V-mesh "nonclimbable" wire, about as expensive per foot these days as stone but incredibly stout and durable in its heavier form. I salvaged some of this from a farm where it had been put up in 1924 and used it to make corrals, which purpose it is now serving well after fifty-odd years in the weather. I know one man who uses it to hold a herd of buffalo—some sort of ultimate test, I should think, for fencing.

Nor shall I deeply explore the subject of electric fences, a highly effective form that is cheap and easy to build and instills an enormous respect, in creatures familiar with it, for anything resembling a stretched wire. A bull, for instance, may touch it once a year with his nose when a heifer in heat is on the other side, but no more often than that. It is no good far from the house in rough country like ours here, for deer and such bang into it and cause shorts and you have to do a lot of trudging to find and fix them. But nearby it is quite handy, besides furnishing much innocent amusement for its owner and his guests when new animals unused to modern conveniences are making its acquaintance. I used to feel guilty about that amusement until I figured out that the reason I laughed was that I had been stung so often by the thing myself.

As this essay may show a bit too fully, what working and worrying with fences over a period of time does to you is to turn you into a fence fanatic. A decade or so ago, a nephew of mine spent the summer of his seventeenth year building fences here on the place, laboring hard and well and often alone, for I had other work elsewhere. Some years later he told me with a certain note of aggrievement in his voice that the experience had soured his former unthinking enjoyment of pastoral landscapes. Riding along a highway, he would find his attention inexorably drawn to the fences that paralleled it, noting the size and strength of cornerpost assemblies, assessing the height of the goat net or the number of barbed wires used, and passing moral judgment on the unknown human beings who owned them. For all of us fence fanatics know that you can tell a lot about a man by looking at his fences.

It passes, though. We grow a bit more charitable in such matters as other concerns and age begin to shape in us a reluctance to spend whole days with pliers and stretchers in the maintenance of our own wire walls. Whether through mellowness or something else with a harsher name, we develop a bit of doubt that a sag here and there really amounts to all that much, so long as our cattle usually stay at home and other people's usually stay out. And from that point, I suppose, it is but a few short philosophical steps to the outlook of those brothers with their shotgun, or it would be if our front porches were only in the right place.

Building Fever

Nearly anyone with an eye for construction carries about in his head a catalog of architectural gems and oddments seen while driving through one countryside or another, and some of them along his more usual routes get to be old friends. He may even grow a bit possessive and secretive about them; they are his. In Texas alone there are scores of structures that I begin to look for, often unconsciously, long before I come to them on trips—barns that are polygonal or notched into hillsides or otherwise remarkable, courthouses and churches of special flavor, corrals built out of railroad ties or stone or interlaced billets of mesquite, unclassifiable flights of fancy of various kinds, and houses of all sizes and materials notable either for handsomeness or because in their aspect there is embodied someone's idiosyncrasy so sharply assertive that each, for better or worse, is easily distinguishable from any other house the beholder's eye has ever beheld.

Ranches or farms all of whose buildings have a unifying personal imprint of this latter sort on them are not uncommon, and sometimes whole small communities are marked. One of my own pet examples of this is a certain straggling tiny crossroads village in near West Texas—call it Elm Tree. It is the sort of place that used to have its own church and school and ser sta gro and maybe a cotton gin, but has now turned satellite to a county seat a dozen or so miles away, its population sparse and for the most part decrepit, half its scant houses empty beneath decayed roofing, its store and schoolhouse stuffed full of someone's baled hay, its handful of youngsters bused off daily for education elsewhere. It has the strong mark of one man upon it, a probably part-time and almost certainly deceased mason who is to me simply the Mad Arch Builder of Elm Tree, for I have never wanted to stop and inquire about him, preferring to form my own vision of him through his work.

At some point this artisan discovered the Roman arch and fell in love with it. Most of the place's houses that were put up before the early Thirties or so (and few, from the look of things, were put up much after that) show evidence of his obsession, some only in an arcaded porch or walkway, a few in windows and doors as well. As a medium, he favored flaglaid limestone—the sort that is put up on edge in fitted jigsaw hunks rather than bedded flat—and polkadotted it with darker stuff, lining some of his arches with red brick while making others of stone throughout. What appears to have been intended as his masterwork is an unfinished small square stone chapel in the village cemetery. Roofless, its thick concretecored flagstone walls petering out at the top in jagged lichened

serrations, it boasts nonetheless as an entranceway a tall noble round-topped arch eight feet wide, through which a passerby may glimpse the delicate green of the johnsongrass and scrub chittamwood that thrive in cracks of the slab floor within.

Though Elm Tree is not directly on the road to anywhere I usually go, I make a jog to pass through it when I can. It isn't that I really *like* the Mad Arch Builder's work; in truth I lack enthusiasm for walls of peanut-brittle flagwork and prefer thick lintels across the top of masonry openings—and if I ever do try to construct any arches they will probably be of the segmental type, not Roman. But I like the fact of that work's existence and I like the Arch Builder himself as expressed in it, and when I idle past the little graveyard within whose sunbaked precincts he must lie, quite possibly felled by his labors on its shrine, I raise my hand in a salute that is not at all ironic. For we have kinship, he and I.

A lot of other people are kinsmen to him also, especially in the country. Like tetanus, the organism that causes construction fever thrives in rural air and, like mumps, it seems to hit you hardest when you catch it in mature years. A good proportion of countrymen are infected with it early enough in life to build up some resistance to its effects, but others, including many of us who elect as adults to make countrymen of ourselves, come down with cases as violent and lasting as that of the Elm Tree Master.

I know that many townsmen have the urge too, but often the scope within which they can yield to it is rather straitly defined. The need to make a nine-to-five living in town terms doesn't help much, nor does neighbors' conservative disapproval of both the activity itself and the results, when fancy has run a bit wild or execution falls short of intention. Bureaucracy through city building codes and such can raise fat obstacles, and on most town-sized lots even space is a potent limitation, as is the general city belief that plumbing and carpentry and electrification and all that are best left to professionals. In consequence, most urban would-be builders have to nurse their malady in private and to palliate its ravages with the fabrication of barbecue pits and toolsheds. If fortunate, sooner or later they get to "build" a house in the suburbs in the sense of having it built to their taste, and at that point they vent their frustration by hectoring thoroughly all architects and contractors and artisans and laborers in sight.

Not that I would be construed as looking down my nose at people who have things built, as long as whatever it is that gets built has on it the stamp of their preferences and quirks. This essay is more or less about types like me with a need to put things together themselves, but I doubt there is one of us who fails to feel, as the years accumulate and vigor doesn't, some envy of that elder world which endured till a couple of generations ago, when anyone with a little wherewithal and imagination could wave his hands at cheap skilled workmen and make his fancies come true, whether or not he ever got calluses on his own palms. Out of that system came Monticello and many another noble country home, and all those fine "follies" on British estates at which doltish sightseers snicker without seeing the lasting statement of self that they are.

In contrast to the cities, out here beyond the exurban fringe neighbors often live a half-mile away or more behind shielding hills and trees and for the most part want nothing better than to mind their own business while you mind yours. Bureaucratic pickings are too thin to tempt much regulation down upon us, and the services of professionals are scarce and costly enough that we have learned to get along without them most of the time and indeed have grown quite brashly confident in our manual skills, laying stone on stone with aplomb and affixing board to board with arrogant hammer blows.

In us susceptibles, something about the very possession of acreage demands its adornment with structures that certify our presence and will keep on certifying our past presence in time to come. I don't pretend that this is very admirable in philosophical or ecological terms, since it is an extension of the same impulse that has smeared man's mess all over the face of nature throughout the world. But it is a human fact. Once your brain has latched onto the idea that if you had the energy and time, or the money to hire enough workers and machines, you could start building the Tower of Babel all over again on the knoll above your vegetable garden, and nobody on this earth could say you nay, you have undergone a change. Even if you hold to the belief that construction ought to fit into a landscape rather than stand out stark on it, as an incipient builder you have to some degree set yourself against wildness and natural disarray.

The tower, now that we've mentioned one, may be the utmost symbol of this, the manmade finger against the sky that means in part perhaps, toward destiny and disorder and death, what an upthrust finger does mean. I suspect that most of us have a personal tower embedded somewhere in our imaginings, though few of us ever find it standing somewhere or get around to building it for ourselves. I myself have not yet quite given up the notion of a stout limestone affair twenty or thirty feet high on the rise behind our house, its lower portion to serve as storage for ten or fifteen thousand gallons of water but on its top a breeze-haunted study from which its exhausted builder might gaze out vacantly at far horizons. And set back from a gravel road in our county that I drive along fairly often there is a less ambitious but actual embodiment of a similar dream. On the summit of a high conical rock hill clad in cedar stands a wooden hut atop four tall creosoted poles. It was erected by the city man and his son who bought that rough property a few years ago, and I am told it is the only building on the place, with a couple of bunks and a cook-stove for the weekends that they spend there, hauling provisions up on a rope. For them I suppose it serves, in an opposite sort of way, a function similar to that of the crawl-space beneath a friend of mine's house in the city, which he used to frequent in his drinking days. He said he liked it there because he could look out at people and they couldn't look back at him.

The rural owner-builder, as the alternative-lifestyle people like to call him, does have something of a time problem in terms of his usual need to make a living, whether through a job elsewhere that supports him and his family and his country habit, through freelance piecework like welding or writing or fence-building or crafts, or through a willingness and ability to depend on the land itself for his needs—or, as often, through some combination of these. Stones do not get put on stones or boards on boards, alas, in a few odd minutes of odd days. But time does flex better out here and has a less nervous, ticktock, demanding role in daily life than more up-to-date locales have allowed it to assume. Even for jobholders and hard-slogging freelancers, spare time is more likely to be truly spare and not cluttered with social pulls and Little League games and brief-cases hauled home full of frantic papers to occupy the evening until the highballs mercifully make sleep feasible. The live-stock tasks and casual forage farming and fence-fixing and other things that make up most country work in a region like mine all need to be done and done right, but when to do them, within limits, is pretty much up to the doer. Our handful of real full-time farmers, cash row-croppers who have to toil night and day when conditions are right for tillage or planting or harvest, have longish slack periods between such peaks of labor. Few men anywhere, of course, ever find enough time in life for all that they have in mind, even those who have most in mind to sit on a porch and squirt tobacco juice at morning-glory blossoms. But if a countryman wants to do something badly enough he can usually find the time, and needless to say we constructors do badly want to construct.

As for what the things are that we want to construct and how we go about it, they vary as widely as our tastes and our needs and our reasons for getting involved in such activity in the first place. Many just want, at the least cost possible, a functional country house and the functional outbuildings and other things that go with it; they shore up and add on to whatever existing structures there are and, when starting something from scratch, tend to use short-cut contemporary methods or even shorter-cut traditional ones based on the abiding country conviction that anything a two-by-ten will do a two-by-four will do just about as well. On the other hand, some of us builders are of the hell-for-stout school, addicted to thick stone walls if we're strong enough and have more time than most folks, and in carpentry using more and heavier members than are technically required and bracing them to withstand tornadoes. Not a few people choose a piece of country property primarily because of the handsome old buildings that already stand there, restoring them and adding on with love and thought and hard labor. And a sprinkling, usually young and willing to go at the thing full-time for as long as it takes, elect such alternative shapes and methods as domes and yurts and free-form shell concrete, or build intensely personal, often lovely structures out of salvaged materials and native timber and stone free for the taking.

For a certain kind of amateur builder, much time goes into dreaming and planning and draftsmanship. I have sheaves on sheaves of papers tucked away in notebooks and file folders, depicting future projects in detail and representing God knows how many hours of bemused, exhilarating work with T-square and ruler and protractor and pencil. Some date far back, as is shown by the absurdly low cost estimates scribbled on them and reflecting the prices charged twelve or fifteen years ago for building materials. They range in sort from built-in walnut bookshelves and house additions to that squat tower and, most recently, a long, vaulted cellar in the hillside behind the house. To build them all in the years that are left to me, even if I wax fairly optimistic about those years' number, would require the existence of plentiful, happy, dirt-cheap helpers of the sort that the owner-builder of Monticello could count on but not we modern decorators of the landscape. Therefore most of them will very likely never progress from paper to concreteness, but for those that I do get around to, the procedure will be mapped out. Unless I change it when the time comes, as happens more often than not . . .

Others of the sect disdain such stodgy forethought and let their creations grow more or less spontaneously. This seems to be particularly true of amateur stonemasons, at least in our part of the world. Rural Texans are by tradition inclined toward taciturnity both in speech and in other forms of self-expression, but a surprising number of them when turned loose with rocks and mortar will thumb their noses at understatement and let her rip. Besides Elm Tree, I have dozens of other examples of personalized masonry in my mental catalog of things to watch for on journeys. Some are houses compounded of red and white and brown stones and bits of petrified wood and beerbottles and things; others are well-houses or gazebos or wishing wells or dry ornamental fountains or yard walls, one admirable specimen of which (near Evant, Texas, as I recall, though it could be Goldthwaite or San Saba) consists of some huge slabs of thick ledge limestone set up on end and cemented into a footing trench with their abutting irregular edges fitting to perfection.

The intended purpose of some masonry items is not to be discerned, either because they are follies put up for the pure joy of it or because they stand unfinished, maybe forever—

extensive stonework being such heavy slow labor that many a novice practitioner either dies or quits somewhere along the way. One project whose growth I have been watching for seven or eight years has unplumb walls of rounded riverbed stones and is one room deep and quite long, maybe seventy feet by now. It has window and door openings in its highway side and something of the look of an old-style mom-and-pop tourist court, but its ceilings, if they ever go in, will be less than six feet from the floor. Every time I see it a bit more length has been added, and once I had the luck to catch its creator at work when I passed. He was a fierce and precipitate old fellow, to judge by the way he slapped his mortar into place and rammed his stones down on it—and he was, of course, quite short.

Houses are the most relevant buildings for most people, but oddly a good many amateur builders who will tackle a barn or other outbuilding with self-expressive gusto shy away from house construction to the point of inhabiting mobile homes or bringing in professionals to put up for them a suburban-style "ranch house" devoid of any imprint save that of anonymous conformity. To a degree, this has to do with the fact that in our time the houses that are acceptable to most prospective inhabitants, but especially to wives, have stopped being a space enclosed by walls and a roof and equipped with some means of cooking and staying warm, and have become "machines for living," stuffed with complex devices that click and whir and groan, and veined with cables and pipes and ducts. But in large part too it is rooted in the circumstance, also unpalatable to wives, that owner-built homes can take a hell of a while to get finished.

Members of an owner-builder's family, in fact, often get to live in partly unfinished quarters for considerable lengths of time, perhaps for the rest of their lives if they're willing to stick around that long. Sometimes this has to do with money and the owner-builder's frugal determination not to spend it till he has it. More often it has to do with time and the abandonment of, say, unpainted but installed and functional doors and windows and such items for more pressing parts of the job or for the crass pursuit of dollars, after which it is remarkable how quickly the o.-b.'s eyes can cease to focus on those items' incomplete state. Again, it may derive from some things needing to be done before others can be finished, which accounts for the fact that our present living room, the stone cabin which was my first residential project on the place and is now intended to serve ultimately as a library, has no baseboards some sixteen years after its construction because there is no point in cutting and fitting baseboards until the built-in bookshelves are up. . . . And finally there is the grandiosity that sometimes sneaks in on country building schemes unawares and leads an obsessee into visions of four-thousand-odd square feet of higgledy-piggledy living space where he once thought two thousand would be plenty, as indeed it would. Hence on wintry mornings my ladies have to trudge to breakfast, from their bedrooms to the "old house," across an expanse of windswept half-frozen mud where in time there will be, if I last and God is willing, a big living room and a new kitchen.

What is certain about us cousins of the Mad Arch Builder of Elm Tree is that we are rarely bored and never hard up for something to occupy such odd bits of loose time as may confront us. What is less certain is that we spend our loose time wisely, but then obsession has seldom had much truck with wisdom. At any rate, when we depart this vale we will leave a few assemblies of stones and planks about with our own marks upon them, and maybe here and there a tower upthrust against fate. And I for one find it in me to hope that if in distant years someone like me passes by and sees these things, he will pause and examine and then perhaps raise a hand in salute, recognizing the kinship between us.

Meat

At bottom human existence is and ever has been quite gory, even if you leave out wars and feuds and duels and murders and other forms of intra-specific violence. The main shed blood has been that of man's fellow creatures and its flow has been steady and copious; in a sense we have floated on it from where we once were to wherever it is we are now. The by-products of this slaughter—leather, fur, sinew, bone, horn, and all that—have been essential equipment on our voyage all the way down to the Age of Plastics, while the chief thing sought—meat—has been so central to our wellbeing that few of us can think of good food without it.

For there is no more basic element in old human experience

than the killing of other species of animals for their flesh, nor do most of us need to read Robert Ardrey to be convinced of this. The proof is in the eating. Most people like to set their teeth in animal protein, and if a good many of them in the world don't get to do so very often, that isn't so much through preference as because meat and fish and fowl, being in prime demand and a few notches up the food chain, are costly. And every piece that shows up on a dinner table sits there in lucid testimony that some creature died at somebody's hands for the diners' benefit and delectation.

There are still parts of the world, most of them distant from most of us, where people depend in the oldest way on wild meat harvested in wild places. Elsewhere the bloodshed is as heavy as it was among Comanches and Zulus and skin-clad Ice Age Europeans, but it involves mainly domesticated beasts dispatched out of sight and hearing of those who will consume them. Even our butchers seldom slaughter anything any more, that function having been taken over by packing houses that ship out carcasses to be cut up for sale. Except in small towns, the backyard flocks of chickens that used to furnish part of a neighborhood's morning symphony as well as part of its food have vanished, as have goats and the hutches of Belgian hares that people here and there throughout the suburbs once raised to eat. One of my own early recollections of meat-killing is of a man down our street who strung up the young male hares on a fence by their hind legs and gave the coup with a chop of his hand to their napes; some squalled before he whacked them, most piteously to ears that had lately absorbed a reading of *Peter Rabbit*. . . .

There is general feeling among *Peter Rabbit* readers as well as others, I suppose, that the change represents attainment of a higher level of existence. Meat creatures with their manure and noises and ailments and the details of their demise and dismemberment have been banished, along with other troublesome basics such as sewage and old folks and the laying out of corpses, to an invisible realm "out there." And through the paper dollar's purchasing power we move ever nearer, or seemed to be moving until just lately, to that aseptic world shown in TV commercials where happiness dwells in aerosol bombs and panty-hose eggs, food comes precooked on a tray, few people seem to age except into gently beaming dentured grandparents with mild arthritis that is easily soothed by patent remedies, and toilets as well as armpits smell sweet.

All this has influenced country life too, of course, but probably less in terms of food than of other things. The country raises food for sale, and eats some of what it raises even if less than in former subsistence times. Here in Texas, most country places are at least partly dedicated to the nurture of meat animals, and meat-eating countrymen take advantage of that fact, often doing some or all of the work involved in getting creatures from pasture or pen to skillet. In the general absence of help, not many of us slaughter beeves any more, for a thousand-pound steer spraddled dead on the ground is a large daunting hunk of something to have to deal with. Instead, when such a beast is fat enough to suit us, we trailer him to a small-town locker plant to be expertly (sometimes) killed and aged and cut up and frozen. Most swine go this route now too, though the happy and ancient ritual of wintertime hog-killing by large families or cooperating neighbors, with its several squealing victims and its hoists and barrels of simmering scald-water and scrapers and sharp knives and guts-tubs and ash-roasted spleens and draughts of warming whiskey, is not yet entirely obsolete among true countrymen.

Such hog-butchering is necessarily a group job, and individual members of a group that have been doing it together over the years tend to get reputations as especially good stickers or carcass-splitters or whatnot. One friend of mine had an uncle who drank so much on these occasions that he wasn't allowed to do anything but hold a washtub to catch the entrails as the belly was slit and they popped out, and he wasn't much good even at that. "Now?" he would insist, barging in among the flashing knives with his tub and making the pendant carcass swing. "Not yet," they would say and shove him aside, only to be assaulted again a moment later: "NOW?" And as often as not some of the innards would spill in the dirt when he did get to try to catch them.

These matters are not for the squeamish, who are widespread enough nowadays that even much small livestock intended for home consumption—lambs and kids and veal calves and such, and more rarely poultry—is carted off to locker plants to meet its fate out of sight. Nearly all of us shirk the job thus on occasion, either because time presses or for less valid reasons. A big pet wether goat that has turned mean, for instance, needs to be disposed of and has some good meat on him, since he's been gobbling grain and other richness all his life. But he has a personal given name too, and was bottle-fed at the house as a kid, and even if you can nerve yourself to butcher him on the place some members of your family are going to be queasy about his meat upon the table.

Usually they are, that is . . . A fellow I know had a goat of that type which had grown so obnoxious that nobody in the family could go outside without a good stick in hand. He hired a man to come do the killing, not wanting to face it himself, and after the goat had been tethered beneath an oak limb for hoisting after slaughter and the moment of truth was nigh, he shooed his children indoors to avoid traumatization. But when the knife went in they were all peeking out of windows and broke into exuberant cheers; the buttings they had received from old Thomas Whiskers had long since wiped out affection and the throat-cutting represented nothing to them but solid overdue revenge. They ate him with pleasure too.

Sometimes to get around a problem of sentimentality and

revulsion you can work out a swap with somebody else who has a spoiled pet on hand, these being numerous and mostly goats. Or you can grind yours into sausage after slaughter. Goat meat mixed with pork fat and seasoned right makes up as well as venison, maybe better, and the nature of sausage is such as to deflect most feelings but appetite, as witness the popularity of the common weenie among consumers young and old who think they wouldn't be caught dead eating the snouts, lips, navels, and other delicate components that go into this democratic *wurst*.

Pets excepted, there is a good bit of solid satisfaction in butchering an animal raised on your own place and turning him into good meat for yourself and your family and friends. The satisfaction has nothing to do with a "love of killing." In my life I have occasionally met twisted types who seemed to get their kicks that way, either at hunting or with tame beasts, and after discerning this I have stayed good and clear of them. You do the killing as quickly and cleanly as you can, because it is there to do, and you swing the carcass up in the air with a gambrel stick lodged between its hind legs, and then with honed shapely knives you get on with the gutting and skinning and cutting up, and the satisfaction lies in the fact that you are engaged in the very ancient and honorable procedure of providing meat—being able to do it and knowing how and facing all the implications that eating flesh entails.

Oddly, or maybe not, even with something as small and simple to handle as a suckling cabrito it is good to have company with you, and I speak as a usual loner. This isn't a matter of sharing guilt but is ancient too, I suspect, tied in with old tribal ways of sharing out the spoils of a hunt. For hunting— though as a subject it constitutes a bottle of worms that I don't intend to uncork here—is the original activity on which all this meat-getting is patterned, and in its convivial aftermath when quail are being plucked and gutted or deer are being dressed, there is for me much the same feeling I have known, for instance, at old-time, joyous, loud, country hog-butcherings. Now and then I have been invited to places where after a hunt the game was turned over to hirelings for this work, and while sometimes tired enough to be glad of it I have nevertheless felt cheated out of a part of what the day had to offer, the pleasure of a job fully done.

It is, I grant, not a pleasure that everyone seems to be built to enjoy, and I don't suppose there's anything wrong with that. But insofar as I worry about the morality of such things, I see even less wrong with the pleasure itself, at least if the person in question eats meat. Toward conscientious vegetarians I feel much respect, though I am not shaped to share their taboos. But to my fellow carnivores I would suggest that there is a good strong dose of honesty and philosophical completeness in occasional full knowledge of just what meat-eating means, and I don't believe that dose is obtainable wrapped in plastic film in a supermarket bin.

Vin du Pays

The old old yearning toward physical self-sufficiency for families and clans runs strong in uncertain times. Nearly all of us sojourners in the countryside have a medium to large shot of it flowing in our veins, whether we have "returned to the land" or never left it in the first place. Society being complex and many-tentacled, self-sufficiency these days tends to be fragmentary at best, but that doesn't lessen an addict's satisfaction in short-circuiting the Great Machine, cheating the system, rolling his own, and coming up with something he needs and can use, generally at very small cost. No home will ever be more his than the one his hands have erected or restored to beauty and function; no meal will ever fill him more pleasantly full than that dinner in lavish June when every piece of food on the table, save perhaps a little olive oil and salt and such, comes off of his own place.

As for drink on that same table, someone has written also that no wine will ever taste bad that you have made yourself, a statement with a nice ring to it that crops up in books and articles on home winemaking. Unfortunately it is hogwash. Unless the average beginning winemaker has extraordinary luck in the matter of his raw materials as well as in his manipulation of them, and unless he has a very shallow awareness of just how good wine can be, he is going to turn out a certain amount of what even he can recognize as slop. He is going to turn out some potable wine too, whether sooner or later, and when he does he is going to give it the full benefit of any doubt because it is his own, as I do when I tell myself (and sometimes others, to my shame) that a particular early batch of acid red, made by guess and by God from garden grapes of indifferent quality, is better than some wine I have had in Europe—without adding that in far nooks of the Pyrenees and elsewhere, long ago in roaming days, I was served some really awful, tooth-roughening stuff.

But, like doctors, we dabblers in oenology have the privilege of burying our worst mistakes, as the liveoaks around my house can bear witness, their roots having absorbed several libations of fluid judged unfit for human consumption after fermentation and aging. And eventually we grow warier, wiser, and a little better at our craft—or at least I assume from watching others that "we" do, my own experience having been limited and sporadic to date and my growth having reached only the wary, half-wise stage. The idea, of course, is to produce something that people can not only drink but like, and thus far I have turned out only a modest quantity that could be offered to visitors with a fair chance of such a result. Most of it has been mead, honey wine, the stuff our distant Nordic forebears guzzled from bulls' horns and human skulls in warriors' halls in winter, while banging on the table for more roast wild pig and trading poetic recollections of murder and pillage and rape along the Irish coast.

No guest of ours has ever been rendered violent from quaffing this mild beverage, made dry rather than sweet and without any heavy spicing. It is a good table drink, especially with light food. True, it isn't really wine, but then neither are many of the other concoctions that the fermentation mania leads us beginners into brewing out of peaches, blackberries, plums, potatoes, and other organic matter. Sugar plus enzymes yields alcohol plus carbon dioxide, goes the oft-cited equation, crudely put, and anything left over is flavor, which in skilled hands can be manipulated with sometimes surprising success, as when what started out as the juice of parsnips or rhubarb stalks may end up tasting like rather nice dry sherry.

Usually what comes out is less epicurean than that, even if pride of creation can make the average home practitioner give it more benefit of doubt than others are likely to extend. In its purest form, I suppose, this attitude was to be found on the Pacific islands during World War II among dungareed makers of jungle juice, which they fabricated out of canned fruit cocktail or dried prunes or whatever and, waiving other criteria, evaluated purely on jolt. Elsewhere in later years, undoubtedly out of cultural prejudice, I have thought to see the same principle at work in such regional products as retsina and pulque. The applicable equation here seems to be alimentary tract plus alcohol in whatever form but in sufficient quantity yields kick plus eventual headache, and so it has ever been. Crudely put.

And yet, infected with the cosmopolitanism of our time and of whatever reading and travels lie behind us, we amateur fermenters do aspire to more civilized production—i.e., to real wine usually imbibed at least as much for the way it tastes as

for what it does to the taster. Real wine is of course the trans-
muted juice of the grape, that magical simple liquid which the
Greeks said was brought to them by a god, in whose honor
they held great annual orgies, and which otherwise rational
Frenchmen compare to sunshine itself. Imitating it well
through the use of other materials than grapes is very hard—
and rather silly too, since making it doesn't amount to much
or doesn't seem to, as anyone knows who has watched a French
or Spanish or Italian farmer laying in his year's supply. In its
simplest, red-wine form, the process consists of gathering ripe
sweet grapes, mashing them with bare dirty feet or otherwise,
letting the whole mess bubble for some days in a tub before
pressing the juice from the hulls and seeds and fermenting it
still further, and finally sealing it into barrels or big pots or
whole tarred animal skins where it will age before being
bottled, if indeed its creator bottles it at all. The grapes' sugar
has obeyed the equation and turned to alcohol and various
other nice things have happened, and what results is dry table
wine, most often pretty good.

But that simple transmutation is itself a miracle, and nobody
knows this better than your peasant farmer himself, who may
be phlegmatic concerning his wife, fatherland, religion, house,
crops, and practically everything else, but is uncontainably
proud of the wine he has made and will be your brother forever if you drink some and show you like it—a phenomenon
I understand better after having made a little myself. . . . Once
many years ago I went with a friend to the remote village of
his birth on the slopes of the Gredos mountains, west of Ma-
drid. It was August, the time of harvest festivals in those parts,
and the village was a pleasant one where everybody seemed
to have a little usable land and a few animals and enough of
life's necessities to get by well in good years. They put on a
fine fiesta too, with elaborate fireworks at midnight on a ruined
castle's wall, a week-long, never-ceasing dance to the music of

clay flutes under great poplars by a clear swift river, fighting bulls turned loose in the main square to gore some of the town's young bravos and in turn to be hacked and stabbed to death inchmeal with scythes and old swords and other hardware by those vengeful bravos who remained, and all sorts of further glories. But its main feature as far as I could tell was the sampling of other folks' wine.

This wine was made and kept in numerous small caves in a mountainside above the town, some of them natural and others dug out of the dirt and rock centuries before, their entries walled up with stones and stout doors set therein. Each belonged to an individual family. In the cool dusk of their depths big *tinajas*—clay pots shaped like the amphorae of the ancient world but seven or eight feet tall and holding maybe seventy-five gallons each of last year's wine and sometimes wine from the years before—stood in wooden racks against the walls. We clambered from cave to cave, exchanging pleasantries with their owners in the measured formal Castilian and accepting wine drawn from the *tinajas'* spigots into rough earthenware cups without handles, made especially for the fiesta and laid in by hundreds beforehand. Occasionally there were edibles too, bitter olives or little morsels of grilled mutton or fish or sun-cured ham or the like.

Drinking with elbow high, you paid rolling compliments to each wine's particular merits, though in truth with the same grapes and methods prevailing in the whole village there was no great difference from cave to cave in what burbled out of the spigots—honest strong red wine with a bit of an edge to it behind the chill of the mountain earth. In return for the compliments you got more wine and great rough Spanish embraces, and when taking your leave you raised your emptied clay bowl ritually and dashed it against the floor. By the end of the week there was a considerable midden of busted crockery to crunch through on our rounds, and the town had quite a few cases of what the Bible calls redness of eye and wounds without cause, and I had made a lot of new friends whose names and faces I can no longer recall. I remember the name of the village, though, and if ever I get back there I hope it's in August and those pagan pipes are tootling ceaselessly by the river and in the hillside caves wine bowls are being smashed, as most likely they have been smashed since Roman times and before.

Whatever may be your own memories, if any, of Old World peasant friends and their wine, you come up against a couple of hitches when you seek to emulate them by making your own here in Texas or roundabout. The first hitch isn't serious—the fact that behind those peasant farmers' every action lie a couple of thousand years or so of family and cultural experience, whereas behind yours lies only a fervent and ignorant desire to be your own Dionysus. You can get around this trouble handily by reading books and utilizing the soft technology they lay before you, modernity's substitute for traditional "feel." You learn to adjust the grapes' sugar content and acidity and to guard your ripening hooch against spoilage organisms by the use of such things as fermentation locks and Campden tablets. You achieve the clarification of cloudy wine, and you become very edgy about ambient temperatures—a problem in these latitudes where grapes come ripe in summer when the weather is too hot for prime fermenting conditions. (The contemporary answer is airconditioning, though that is hard technology and sits but poorly on the conscience of real self-sufficiency types, who would prefer a cave. . . .) And thus in time you stand a chance of reaching a point where you can more or less consistently make the most, or anyhow not the least, of your raw materials' potential.

But those raw materials themselves, the grapes, are the really big sticking point for most of us American would-be peasants, or have been till just lately. What our counterparts across the water have to work with is one variety or another of the Old World wine grape, *Vitis vinifera*. In this country, because of harsh winters and various diseases and parasites, that supreme and proven species grows well only in California and a few restricted patches of territory elsewhere, as wine-minded agriculturalists from the time of Thomas Jefferson and before have had to learn the hard way. So the average American winemaker, if bored with elaborating jungle juice, has usually had to depend on the wild grapes that grow in profusion all over the continent or on tame varieties derived from them, the so-called American bunch grapes like Concord and Delaware. They make good juice and jelly, but their wine on the whole is disappointing by accepted standards. It can be and often is sweetened into kosher-type or "pop" wine that isn't much different from jungle juice of whatever origin, though when disseminated commercially along with California port and tokay it does serve the social function of keeping Skid Row soddenly content except on mornings-after, when sodden discontent sets in.

Here in Texas, with its physical breadth and its spectrum of climates and soils, more species of wild grapes occur than anywhere else on the continent, and a corresponding diversity of tame types can be grown. In parts of the Trans-Pecos region in the west even European vinifera will thrive, having been grown around El Paso since Spanish days, though I'm told the old winery there has folded. At the opposite end of things, in forested damp East Texas, the Southern muscadine reigns, another sweet-wine grape. And in between where most of us live, a little bit of everything else can be found, subject to the vagaries of soils and germs and rots and fungi. From all these grapes wine has been made since Caucasians first showed up—good, bad, or indifferent wine, though mainly alas of the latter two types.

The species most entangled with Texas tradition is the wild

mustang grape, whose thickstemmed vines with drooping umbrella-like leaves deck trees and fences throughout the central regions of the state from the Red to the Rio Grande. To arriving Germans in the Hill Country a hundred and thirty years ago, those vines with their big dark grapes looked like a gift from *Herr Gott*, for among immigrants to Texas these were the champion self-sufficiency enthusiasts of all time, fresh from European peasant traditions and wanting their own wine more ardently than any of us moderns can. Their Heaven-directed gratitude, I am certain, must have crumbled badly when the time came to taste the first vintage of mustang red, whose characteristic acidity, unless masked behind a good bit of added sugar or otherwise ameliorated, is enough to tie an unwary drinker's tongue into fancy turk's-head knots. Chronicler "Texas John" Duval, a contemporary of these Teutons, claimed to have once brewed up a large commercial batch of this wine that blistered and twisted the rubber boots with which he had equipped his grape tramplers and in the end couldn't be sold because "all who sampled it said it was too sour for vinegar and too fiery for aquafortis."

But the hill Germans were and are a persistent folk, and eventually they learned to cope with the mustang grape's worst qualities and ended by shaping a sort of tradition around its wine. Even after tame grapes (not very good ones, true) adapted to the region's peculiarities were found and brought in, plenty of people there kept on making the mustang red. Most of us who have frequented those hills have tried it, and many of us have made some on our own. The best is more or less sweet, and of most it can be said, as of the illicit white whiskey that used to be distilled in these other more northerly limestone hills where I live, that it's not bad if you haven't got anything else to drink.

Now, however, the good tame grapes are here, or seem to

be. Here and there and elsewhere. Nearly everyone with any interest in the subject has heard about them by now—the "new" French-American hybrid wine grapes that have been spreading by fits and starts in this country since their commercial introduction, in the late 1940's, by Philip Wagner of Baltimore. Their potential has been a basic motivating force behind the establishment of scores on scores of new wine-oriented vineyards, amateur or commercial, in many hitherto improbable places like Ohio, Virginia, Arkansas, Wisconsin, and Texas. Another strong factor, of course, has been the growth of wine drinking and the rise in demand and prices, as more and more Americans have found out what they've been missing.

These hybrid grapes, in an almost bewildering number of varieties adapted to different conditions and purposes, have been under development in France since the last century, one outgrowth of the panic that hit the European wine industry after accidentally introduced American parasites and ailments nearly wiped it out. They are in steady use over there for making not great but good, acceptable wine. At their best they combine the climatic hardihood and disease resistance of our native species with much of the winemaking quality of the old Dionysian vinifera, and they're doing well just about everywhere they've been tried in the U. S., thank you, except so far north that the growing season won't give them time to ripen, and in sections of the South where endemic curses like Pierce's disease let only muscadines prosper.

In Texas much of the publicity given them so far has had a hoop-de-doo commercial tone: plant grapes and get rich. It has centered mainly on the South High Plains around Lubbock, where some painstaking experimentation is under way, but other nodes of hopeful activity exist or are shaping up here and there in other parts of the state. Beyond the Pecos and thereabouts there is a parallel growth of new interest in vinifera culture. Optimism is coldwatered from time to time by sober analysts who point out that it took Europe many centuries to evolve its really great grapes adapted to restricted, often tiny regions and to develop fine wines from them, while California is still learning after nearly three hundred years of viticulture. So even with a scientific approach it could be a good span of years before we have any idea of the ultimate potential of wine grown and fermented in Texas—or in Arkansas or Virginia or Missouri. And it may be a few more years than that before people start getting rich out of the process, if many ever do.

Somehow, though, I doubt that when the dust all settles getting rich will prove to have been the main point. In a muted and small-scale but probably significant way, what appears to be on the verge of happening here has some resemblance to the introduction of *Vitis vinifera* itself into Europe from its Middle-Eastern homeland back in prehistory, whether it was brought by a god or just by some migratory bibbers. Large parts of North America are being quietly furnished with material for making native wine of adequate quality, and some is already being made. Honest wine taken in moderation is food like bread and cheese and meat, and has been prized forever as a staple blessing in all lands where wine grapes could be grown. It seems dubious that for all our present shrill urbanism and our insulation from earthy things we are different enough from other men to turn down something, when offered, that has meant as much as good daily wine has always meant. I suspect that in time—and what after all is time to the vines, once here?—a new and perhaps gentling element will creep into American life, born of the activities of thousands of vineyardists and winemakers, some professional but most amateur or part-time, some hoping to cash in big but more doing it for a little extra money or simply because they want to, who now are and in the future will be feeling out the possibilities of these grapes and their offshoots in different regions and climates.

Yes, I've got mine started, something over a hundred vines of seven varieties, planted last spring, of which six varieties are doing fine and the other has gone chlorotically yellow and stayed that way despite applications of iron and potassium, but I expected more trouble than that in this limestone soil of mine. If in the long run just two sorts do well here, say one good red and a white, I will have what I was after and will toast my friends in my own solid wine when they come out to visit. There might even be a cave as well wherein to do the toasting, for I have been studying out the possibility of gouging a great slot in the hillside behind the house with a bulldozer, then building a long stonewalled cellar in it to be covered over with thick cool earth.

Maybe in a few years we can smash some clay bowls there.

Trash as Treasure

When a personal habit or attitude starts showing up with fair
regularity in your dreams, I suppose you have to consider it
ingrained for better or worse. Not long ago, after a latish
supper involving cornbread, raw onions, blackeyed peas
cooked with cayenne peppers and fat salt pork, and some
leftover chocolate mousse, I had a mild nightmare about being
closely pursued from building to building of a shattered city
by a squad of alien soldiers dressed in queer medieval uniforms
but armed with automatic rifles. While scrambling on all fours
through rubble from one ruined structure to the next, I came
to a crater in which were exposed some broken electrical lines
with attached conduit connectors and service-entrance heads

and other such equipment. And despite the urgent hostile voices and footsteps behind me, and my fear, I stopped and began prying things loose and unscrewing them and ramming them into my pockets. They were much too good and useful to be left behind.

While I've never come close to attaining that degree of parsimony in waking life, I can discern in myself such a tendency as the years progress, and I know pretty well where it comes from. Its main source undoubtedly is the fact that I've led a country life during most of the past two decades, for among us brethren of the ruddy neck, savingness and salvage have never lost their currency, a main theme I will come back to presently. It derives too from having been a writer for thirty years, not highly productive and only occasionally salaried; such a rogue specimen learns early in the game that for him any economic system is a jungle red in tooth and claw, and he either gets used to the idea of living sparely and making do with little when he has to, or else finds a more comfortable direction for his energies. And farther back still, this miserly inclination is rooted in experience with some fairly hard times in the Thirties, when I was growing up.

I can't claim truly proletarian origins, but during my late childhood and adolescence one would have needed tunnel vision and a quite rudimentary brain to stay unaware that things were very tough around and about, and to see extravagance as anything but a path to trouble and woe. Furthermore, a continuity with past human experience still existed strongly in those days, and my people like most others had collective remembrance of even harder times in country places and small towns, tracing back to Reconstruction, to the rich but frugal frontier, to the Old World and its ways. There were wasters and spendthrifts among us, but not many. People hung onto what they had, if they had anything, and trash collectors in our town had much smaller loads of stuff to worry with, on a customer per-capita basis, than members of that calling do today.

On the other hand, as citizens of a land that was still rather lavishly endowed with good things despite its occasional bouts of economic constipation, neither were most of us much inclined toward compulsive scrimping and salvaging, which we tended even during a depression to view as humorous. In our funny papers we had the Toonerville Trolley's Old String Saver to laugh at, and in my neighborhood we had a quiet gentleman who suddenly conceived a passion for used jars and bottles, which he could not bear to throw away and indeed fished out of other people's garbage cans on frequent sorties along our alleys with a towsack, wearing a doublebreasted suit and a tie. They stood in serried, sparkling, multicolored ranks on shelves he had built for them along his back fence, outlined his flowerbeds and walkways, filled a disused servants' room attached to the garage, and finally started creeping on little cat feet into the house, at about which point his family (bottles not being the only problem) committed him to the veterans' mental facility at Waco and hired two elderly black men with a mule and a small beat-up wagon to tote off the vitreous accumulation. These haulers worked at their task for two or three days, chiefly because they were a bit touched with bottle-mania themselves and handled and loaded every item tenderly to avoid breakage, which took some doing with a springless iron-wheeled vehicle.

Our amusement over something like that was nonetheless a bit wry, for we recognized it for what it was. It was just a funhouse-mirror magnification and distortion of the old waste-not-want-not frugality in which a majority of us Americans then believed, whether or not we practiced it all the time. We were laughing at ourselves, and at the rural past that underpinned our ways.

World War II marked the end of those times and the apparent end of some other things too. In the economy of throwaways and planned obsolescence that evolved after it wastefulness became a national virtue, a force that kept factories and businesses humming and created both jobs and wealth. It created a lot of pleasure of a sort also, freeing the general population from old restraints like a preacher's pretty daughter turned loose in a strange and delectably sinful city, though marvelously there was no need to feel guilt. Buying a new Thunderbird you didn't need with money you didn't have, you could if you wished work up a glow of righteousness over your part in helping to maintain—nay, increase—the GNP.

In recent years, of course, doubt has replaced a good many people's righteous glow as the price of the gallon of gas that will propel a T-Bird about nine or ten miles down the pike has edged up past a dollar toward God knows what stopping place, erstwhile desert raiders grow richer than very rich Texans, heat sometimes fails to gush from heating ducts, rivers and even breezes smell bad, and fish sticks arrive at table impregnated with tasty carcinogens. Our tenure in sinless Eden begins to seem less assured, and here and there among the fruit trees stand prophets calling themselves environmentalists, ecologists, post-industrialists, and other things, who assert loudly that there really is guilt after all. They cry out, these spoilsports, for a return to thriftiness on a grand scale— for husbandry of resources, for scrimping and patching and saving, for salvage and re-use which in current prophet language are known as recycling.

Well and good, an aging rustic observer thinks. Very well and very good, in fact, and high time it was for such ideas to grab ahold. But in his innocent mind there is a glimmer of the déjà-vu: he puzzles, this peasant naïf, over whether there is really much difference between these rather modish activities mobilized beneath the banner of ecology, and a lot of ancient practices and attitudes that have limped along with our species through the centuries under a crude tattered ensign labeled Need. Men have always rejoiced in extravagance when luck permitted, from primitive yahoos harrying entire herds of bison over a cliff for the sake of a few steaks and chops, to modern suburbanites generating X pounds of rich garbage per head per day and vacationing in Las Vegas. But that sort of luck has been rare, and the salient economic traits of the bulk of humankind through history have been thrift and stingy inventiveness, which still rule supreme across most of the earth's curving crust. What he wonders, our old déjà-viewer, is whether the present uproar doesn't just mean that the tortoise is catching up with the hare, that some age-old gritty facts of life are getting ready to reassert themselves against the prodigal way of being that a few Western nations have been able for a time to afford.

For in rural regions of even the Western world those facts have never sunk beneath the surface of things. At rare and uncertain intervals farmers and graziers have managed to gather a little of boom's largesse along with their city cousins, but more normally they have had to watch from afar, wistfully or at times with rage, the major harvest of cash and its attendant fun and games. While most care enough for their life on the land to stick it out there if they're able, large numbers of them, especially among the small-timers, have been forced to leave by an inability to pay for the highpriced goods and equipment they either need or have been seduced into buying, and often also by the rebelliousness of wives and offspring who find the antiseptic and pleasure-filled world they see on TV preferable to the labors, stinks, and simplicities that a country existence traditionally entails.

Survivors therefore are likely to be types who have chosen sturdy mates and are willing to work at outside jobs when country income dwindles. They also have a high resistance to the charm of expensive shiny machines and gadgets, and above all they are imbued with the old rural instinct and ability to patch and salvage and improvise and substitute whenever possible, instead of buying. Frugality has never gone out of style for them; they wear it like a much-darned sweater.

Nowhere is this more apparent than in marginally productive country like these rocky cedar hills where I live, and in no way is it better shown than in the hill-dwellers' prevalent attitude toward materials that an industrial society gone mad regards as trash, waste, junk. What much trash amounts to around here is a potential defense against the demons of a hostile economy; it serves not only to repair one's machines and other possessions and to keep them usable but also to fabricate new ones. One or another kind of it fits into tractors, implements, buildings, plumbing systems, fences, feeders, or elsewhere, and if it doesn't fit anywhere it probably has some wondrous new country usefulness of its own, just waiting to be discovered. Hence the durable forms of it are seldom treated with the contempt they get in cities, where they're tossed out to be whisked away by municipal employees for destruction or burial at distant sites, but are saved, often cherished, and given new purpose when occasion permits.

In truth it sometimes seems that the ability to amass junk and to use it ingeniously is a measure of true countryness, not only among natives but among part-timers like me and even some of the well-heeled city people who for a good many years have been buying and fixing up old homestead tracts in our hills, at first for weekend pleasure and then, as fascination progresses, for use as stock farms or little ranches. With these latter the use of trash may begin as an amusing way to emulate local picturesqueness—old tractor seats made into patio stools and so on—but it generally gets more earnest as they discern what a fathomless pit of expenditure the improvement and working of a country place can be unless you learn to cut corners. And when they start being proud of their junk like the rest of us, they are snared for good.

I lately examined a fine cordwood splitter designed and constructed by a friend of mine. Among its components were a five-horse aircooled engine from a wrecked lawnmower, a Case tractor's hydraulic pump, a long-stroke piston out of the landing gear of a World War II bomber, two lengths of railroad track, a massive riving wedge made from old plowshares welded together, and various other hunks of metal gleaned with a cutting torch or a wrench from car frames and elsewhere. Such mechanical complexity is beyond my own modest powers, but I found it admirable, just as its maker understands my pride in more rudimentary creations like watertroughs fashioned from the galvanized drums of big cable spools, and an efficient grape-crusher with rollers made out of lengths of leftover plastic sewer pipe, some pulleys and bearings from a wornout washing machine, and a handle off of a busted meatgrinder.

Bomber parts and cable spools and railroad iron are obviously not typical run-of-the-mill rural refuse. Neither are crossties, public urinals, car driveshafts and axles and engine blocks, used telephone poles, oilfield sucker rods and drill-stem pipe, anchor chains, highline brace cables and earth screws and eyebolts, howitzer wheels, fire-escape ladders, street paving bricks, signboards, janitors' sinks, steel barrels, landing mats, and a good many other sorts of technological detritus that find their last, sometimes bizarre employment out here among us hayseed inheritors. With them we supplement our local sources of trash, which are often meager precisely because of all the indigenous frugality and the repair skills that keep things functioning practically forever.

We find them in the automotive cemeteries, junk and wrecking yards, war surplus emporia, and other cluttered trash havens of the cities, where so much discarded treasure finds a resting place. On trips to town we may browse for hours in favorite establishments of this sort, like bookworms on the quays of Paris, emerging most often with a few irresistible artifacts in the beds of our pickups, acquired for a pittance and perhaps not even needed now, but far too good to pass up. Without this copious fountainhead of exotic refuse I am sure we would feel deprived, as some apolitical Korean and Vietnamese peasants—crafty junk-utilizers, both breeds— must have felt when the prodigious flow of GI waste slacked off in their respective lands. Maybe we would form our own cargo cults as certain Melanesian tribesmen have done in hazed recollection of war's richness, awaiting with drums and prayer and a rattling of boar-tusk bracelets the airborne return of the lavish alien god John Frum.

Singing my song of trash, I sense the onset of shudders in more esthetic readers, who may recall country dooryards where defunct cars and appliances and large objects of rusty iron vied with lilac bushes and shade trees and views of distant hills for an observer's attention, and who conclude that such scenes must be the inevitable effect of a fascination with junk. It is not so. True, some collectors do get to thinking that their prizes are pretty all by themselves, but their wives seldom share the belief, and most country junk awaits its time of resurrection in repositories out of sight of the house. My own supply, for instance, is divided between an area behind the barn, where heavy or "valuable" things molder in dignity, and our household dump in a stabilized gully across the creek, where more portable and ordinary pieces rear up out of a sea of cans and glass and plastic and crumpled baling wire. (Shamefully and unecologically we burn most paper and such, though organic kitchen waste goes to the garden to be plowed under like manure.) But it's *there* if I ever want it, and even if I can't always find a needed item by delving into my own assortment, I can often cadge one or trade for it—the swap being another prime element in rural thrift—from out of a neighbor's hoard.

As for the deliberate decorative use of junk *qua* junk, once common in our Texas landscape, it has fallen off sadly in recent decades as homogenized electronic sophistication has infiltrated people's consciousness. I refer to such things as yard fences made from dummy practice bombs or landing mats or bedsprings or cultivator wheels, and flowerbeds ringed with old truck or tractor tires painted red, white, and blue. Examples of this kind of work are rare enough now that I get a nostalgic twinge from their sight, and though I know very well that a current vogue in the use of native natural materials like cedar poles and limestone is in far better taste, I still sometimes find myself missing certain striking monuments to some junk lovers' conviction that trash is glorious stuff. One of these was the home of an obviously vigorous and probably Rabelaisian family in a small central Texas town I used to pass through on trips. At the perimeter of its lot was a ten-foot levee of tamped sodded earth on top of which they had embedded a parapet of old stoves, refrigerators, washing machines, and toilet bowls, these last being filled with artificial flowers. It was something to look forward to, but my last time through I saw that they had moved away and a philistine new owner had had their fortress razed flat with a bulldozer.

Those of the rest of us who let our affair with refuse escape from the realm of its usefulness mainly manage now to confine the visible result to a knickknack shelf or two full of old

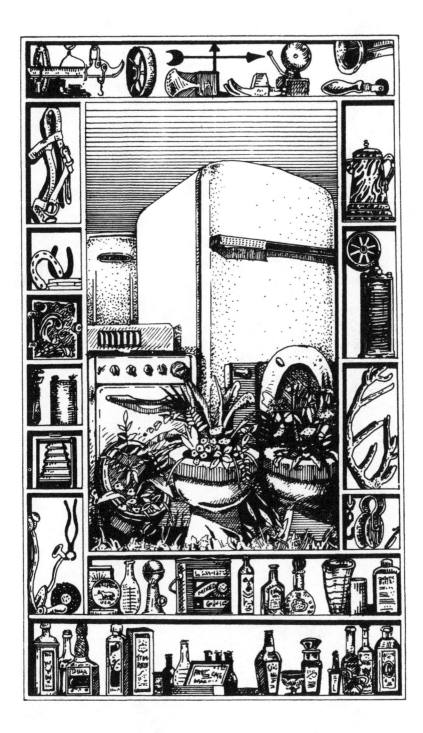

cough-syrup bottles, rusty spurs, harness buckles, fragments of Model T Fords, shed deer antlers, and other such delights found here and there on our property. But there's always danger the thing can get out of hand. Not long ago, after planting my little French-hybrid vineyard, I started looking ahead to its time of fruitfulness and told a few city friends of gourmet bent that I'd appreciate their saving wine bottles for me. They did so with a vengeance, and at present their response lies several layers deep in a small separate shack we call "the bunkhouse" and has invaded a side room of our home. The accumulation is causing uneasiness in the family's senior female, but as for me I find all these jewel-like, flat-bottomed bubbles of glass exquisite, quite aside from their intended purpose. I soak off their labels, wash them till they gleam and glitter, dry them upside down in a rack, plug their mouths with tissue against dust and web-weaving spiderlets, and then sort them according to hue and shape—burgundy, claret, rhine, or italianate oddball—before stowing them away in compartmented cartons liberated from a liquor store's garbage.

As the stacks of cartons grow I find myself gloating over them, and only now and then do I wonder idly who it is, far back in the mists of my youth, that I remind myself of. . . .

Kindred Spirits

I have what started out as a canvas-covered wooden canoe, though with the years it has taken on some aluminum in the form of splinting along three or four fractured ribs, and this past spring I replaced its rotting cloth rind with resin-impregnated fiberglass. It is thus no longer the purely organic piece of handicraft that emerged from a workshop in Maine some decades back. Nor do I use it more than occasionally these days, to run a day's stretch of pretty river or just to get where fish may be. Nevertheless I retain much fondness for it as a relic of a younger, looser, less settled time of life.

While readying its hull for the fiberglass I had to go over it inch by inch as it sat on sawhorses in the barn—removing the mahogany outwales and stripping off the old canvas, locating unevennesses in the surface of the thin cedar planking, sanding and filling and sanding again so that protuberances and pits would not mar the new shell or lessen its adhesion, and finally taking out the seats and thwarts and readying the interior for fresh varnish. The process took up a good bit of my spare time for weeks, and during it I got to know a couple of Indians fairly well. At least I thought of them as Indians, for the canoe company which takes its name from the Old Town of the Penobscots used to employ many of that tribe's members as workers, and for all I know still does.

There was the Good Indian, as I came to call him, who had stood on the left side of the craft while it was being built ("port" and "starboard" will not serve, for the thing had lain sometimes rightside up on its trestle or table or whatever had held it, and sometimes upside down), selecting and trimming his planks with care and affixing them to the ribs so that their edges and butts fitted tightly and the tacks were driven precisely flush, drilling his screw and bolt holes true. And across from him on the right side had labored his confrere Slovenly Pete, a brooder and a swigger of strong waters during the long Maine winter nights, who with reddened eye and palsied hand had messed up everything he could without getting fired from his job. Their ghosts were with me, and I spoke to them as I went over their work and did my own. The Good Indian was a friend, a taciturn perfectionist in sympathy with my resolve to get things right. But somehow I took more interest in his shiftless mate, a sour and gabby type who responded to my gibes about hammer marks and ill-matched planks and protruding tackheads with irrelevant rhetoric on white men's viperish ways, or biting queries as to what business a Texan had fretting over a canoe in the first place. "Your God damn rivers," he said at one point, "ain't got no God damn water in them most of the God damn time."

I've been in this sort of touch with many artisans and laborers over the years, for I am both a putterer and a country-man, categories of humanity that frequently busy themselves in refurbishing and repairing things that other human beings have made or refurbished or repaired in times gone by, leaving personal imprints on them. An old Ford tractor, for example, whose hydraulic pump was replaced by a previous owner with a second one from another model, by dint of much ingenious grinding and shimming and drilling, can cause one to ponder and blaspheme for days over the question of why the costly new pump he has driven fifty miles to buy at a dealership can't be seated. And if, when starting casually to pull out a decayed forty-year-old fence cornerpost set four feet deep, in order to put a new one in its place, you discover that whoever installed it was such a fence nut that he filled the hole around it with angular crushed road gravel tamped down to grip like death, your emotions are mixed as you strive without success to budge his monument with a tractor drawbar or a jack rated at five thousand pounds' lift. On the one hand you have to admire the uncompromising correctness that made him go to such trouble; on the other, more strongly, you wish that in the matter of fence strength he had been a bit more of a slob, like yourself.

Sweatily romantic couples who have redone, maybe rebuilt, old houses with their own hands, ripping out ancient wall-paper and linoleum and pipes and wiring and such, searching out pockets of dry rot and settled foundation piers and chim-ney cracks, working everything down to bare wood and masonry or beyond, nearly always arrive at intimacy with their predecessors in those abodes, their Good Indians and Slovenly Petes. Nearly always too they find the villains more interesting than the nice guys. It is, of course, most pleasant to learn that underneath some textoned plasterboard and eight or ten layers of bargain-basement latex paint and wallpaper and white lead and alligatored varnish and the like, you're the owner of a room paneled in wave-grained solid black walnut beautifully fitted and joined, or that above the rusty stamped-tin ceilings of a stone Hill Country cabin are beams of native post oak hewn square with an adze by some ancestral Deutscher. But it's probably a bit more fascinating to discover, as a friend of mine did, that the faint stink which has seeped for years from a north kitchen wall and has lately grown too stout to ignore derives from the grassroots inventive genius of an anonymous former occupant who insulated that wall by filling its stud spaces with cottonseed hulls, fermented now by a siding leak into rich and miasmic silage.

One has to face also from time to time some effect or the other of the powerful belief, among Prairie Gothic carpenters of a more innocent era, that a two-by-four would serve for just about any purpose. I've seen whole upper floors sustained by joists of those dimensions, a bit concave and springy underfoot but still functional, and in one antiquated farmhouse that my wife and I rented cheaply for several years because we were willing to refinish it ourselves, I traced some mysterious cracks and sags to a small bracket built out of five or six short lengths of two-by-four yellow pine nailed halfway up the wall of a closet and sheathed in shiplap. It held up an entire brick woodstove flue that must have weighed, according to my rough computation, about 4500 pounds avoirdupois. I had strange feelings about that chimney and the ghost who'd put it there, and I hoped that whenever it fell it would choose to collapse straight down toward where its foundation ought to have been, rather than topple sideways through the attic and ceiling onto the bed where gentle sleep enveloped us or the table where we ate. But now, nine years after we moved out of that house and maybe sixty or seventy after the chimney was erected, I note with interest whenever I drive along that road that it is still poking up quite vertically above the roofline, and in fact wintertime wisps of smoke tell me that a current tenant enamored of alternative energy has hooked up a woodstove to it again.

Living now on this place we have owned for two decades where I have built all the structures, sometimes with help but often not, the ghost I most usually have to confront is myself. A chimney that leaks at its flashings, an outbuilding set up on blocks of wood through which termites have made a gleeful invasion, a sheet-iron barn roof that siphons rainwater at some seams when certain winds are blowing, a crawl-space inundated by storms through the place where waterpipes enter— all these joys and others are traceable not to the faulty theories or sloppiness of old-time carpenters and masons but to my own apprentice ignorance. An owner-builder lives with his botches, and working to correct them he waxes introspective, not necessarily with admiration.

I seldom work up the guts for that ultimate form of puttering which involves the patching or restoration of good antique furniture and other classic artifacts. Stout, relatively crude, country-made relics, whose charm is in their honesty and in the sheen of long hard use, I will tackle willingly enough, for the stout crude honest repairs that befit them are within my capacity and their native woods and other materials are usually easy to match. But it takes naïveté or a special sort of arrogance to tamper with the civilized products of vanished masters' vanished dexterity with hand tools. Their aged and chip-prone hardwoods, harvested perhaps in distant forests of the old British Empire where tigers burned bright and white men carried a metaphoric burden and dark men a literal one, are very hard to duplicate with inserts or patches made from woods available now. Furthermore the powered machines on which most present woodworkers depend won't reproduce the contours of their moldings and furbelows, and authenticity prohibits the use of epoxies and other miracle fillers and cements, mainstay substances in modern repair. Bungled work can lower their often considerable value, so like most other people I'm usually willing to leave restoration to professionals or to let the wounded things sit in their corners as is.

Spirits inhabit them too, of course, those of their gifted makers in the individual organic perfection of their shaping and joining and decoration, those of intermediate Slovenly Petes in crude repair jobs undertaken at some point in their history and showing up now as ill-seated reinforcement blocks and screwdriver nicks and other defects. And if one does let arrogance tempt him into essaying such a job himself, as I have on rare occasions, more often than not he ends up leaving a Slovenly Pete spoor also, or else giving up in the middle and either abandoning the object in question in a dismantled state or letting somebody else puzzle it back together. Sometimes with a flush of guilt I run across envelopes or cartons with labels on them in my own handwriting such as "Trim from dressing room bureau" or "Pieces of rosewood snuffbox." This latter project hit a dead end some eleven years ago when I was unable to find any nickel silver of the right thickness for making a new delicate hinge to replace a broken one, and then it got forgotten in a round of very different puttering, the framing of a barn. I do still intend to seek out that metal and finish up the job, though, maybe in tremulous old age when my chances of being a Slovenly Pete will be even better than now.

In addition to being a putterer with things, I find with some surprise, having spent much of my younger life avoiding ownership when I could, that I have turned into a hoarder of them too. Marriage and parenthood are partly to blame, I guess, and country life even more. At any rate the owned objects that surround us now—some still serving a good purpose, some serving none at all, others awaiting a time of use or donation to somebody else—form massive clutters in workshop and office, and pile up in attics and on platforms under the barn roof and in any odd corner of our house and outbuildings that stays unoccupied for more than a week or so. I do sometimes muse out pleasurable fantasies of setting some large fires or holding a huge garage sale and then driving away with my mate to a spare life aboard a small ketch in coastal waters, but the fact is that I seem to be stuck with these belongings in a complex way. They *belong* where they are just about as much as I do, and if some morning I were to walk into the barn and note that an accustomed item was not there—say the battered Rube Goldberg seed cleaner that I picked up at a farm auction and use maybe once in three years, between which times it sits there stolidly collecting mud-dauber nests and goat-manure dust and blocking passage—I would feel my little world's foundations shudder slightly.

Undoubtedly the main trouble is that nearly all these impedimenta have spirits in them by now, either for me or my wife and daughters or simply for themselves. They were made by somebody, even if that somebody was only a stamping-machine jockey in some dark satanic mill of Pittsburgh or Chicopee Falls. Most bear marks of human use and misuse, and some, of the sort one starts accumulating as older relatives die off and one becomes an older relative oneself, have family stories and meanings attached to them. Heavy tables and sets of shelves put together by my late father, an inveterate putterer himself, tools and World War I stuff of his, a great-grandfather's gargoyled notary seal, large brass-latched Bibles with genealogical scribblings that omit most data about miscreants and black sheep, the cow's-horn cup that Great Uncle Billy Cavitt whittled out for his little sister, my grandmother, as he lay in a tent hospital getting used to the absence of a leg shot off at Pleasant Hill, the thirty-two that Grandpa bought for defense against a gambler in Cuero after a horse-whipping in which Grandpa had wielded the whip . . .

Others recapitulate past bits of my own existence and if, as has been claimed, the unexamined life is not worth living, I suppose they serve a useful end. Certainly if one has made a good many haphazard changes of direction in his lifetime it is at least instructive every now and then, after a certain point, to catch a glimpse of something that one was before. The Old Town canoe carries freight like that, along with its spectral red crew. An earring from an early love's rosy lobe can still rowel memory, as can things like a Boy Scout hatchet, still good, a set of blackened silver lieutenant's bars, or a curious brass halyard snap given me long ago by a sailing friend in Mallorca and used now as a paperweight. A volume of James Branch Cabell, encountered lately in rummaging, made me pause and wonder over the very young me who admired and imitated his work, thank God without publishing the results, and a moth-tattered collection of trout flies that I tied up my-self nearly thirty years ago, nymphs and wet flies and dries in all manner of patterns and sizes, brought back with freshness a compressed and separate parenthesis of time spent in a high valley of the Sangre de Cristo. I lived there alone for six months in a spruce-log shack rented from a rancher-Penitente, wrote earnest confused stories about the war, went down to Santa Fe for supplies and carousal when I felt like it or needed to, and with absorption fished the pools and riffles of a crystal alder-shaded creek either by myself or with an old and close and troublesome friend who would drive up from Albu-querque on weekends. Except that one Friday night he made a few bars before setting out and at two o'clock in the morn-ing his car flipped over in the desert near a place called Gal-isteo and that was all of that, but I and the moth-gnawed Royal Coachmen and Bivisibles remain.

Freight enough . . . Despite everything, there does still

dwell in me a remnant of that fellow who didn't want to own things, and for sanity on occasion I'm glad to know he's there. Sometimes he rears up and asserts himself and I muster the nerve to throw out a few cartons and sacks and pickup loads of unusable gear, or give them away, or burn them. But then the spirits start squeaking and gibbering in rage (ours do seem to make such noises, like Elizabethan spirits: not for them the quavering moan of midnight grade C movies) and I stay my hand before matters go too far. For it is well known among devotees of the occult that offended spirits are much less easy to live with than unoffended ones. And if one lives in a world dominated by things, how shall he know what spirits lurk where?

Creatures

Nineteen Cows

Standard agricultural publications and the farm-ranch pages of our Sunday newspapers tend to be condescending toward small-scale cattle raisers, as indeed they are toward small-scale anybody else in this age of agribusiness, or agri-bigness as someone has called it. Only the other day I ran across a slighting reference, in an interview with a Texas A. & M. professor who was touting the recycling of used Baggies into feedlot rations or something on that order, to "people that have nineteen cows." It stung a bit, for I usually have only a few more cows than that myself—rarely in excess of about thirty-five, with a bull and varying numbers of attendant offspring from year to year. But it didn't sting very much, because no learned

Aggie could possibly wax more brilliantly caustic about my relationship to bovines than I have waxed about it myself when a bad winter or a drouthy summer has made tending them an onerous daily concern, or when the market for calves, as frequently, is so miserable that any owner who can count on his fingers can see clearly that they're costing him more to raise than there's any chance of recouping when he sells them as his land's major product.

And yet, despite occasional resolves to get rid of the whole herd and to let the land revert to brushy wildlife habitat where I might stroll unconcerned bearing gun or fieldglass or just a set of appreciative feelings toward nature in her magnificence, such as it is around here, I'm still saddled with my quota of these large and fairly stupid beasts about a decade and a half after buying the eight weanling Angus heifers that were the mothers and grandmothers of my present bunch. Nor does it seem too likely that I'll break loose from them unless I manage to break loose from the land itself, a possibility that I think about fondly from time to time when country life grows cluttered and demanding. For the cattle, unnumerous and marginally economic though they may be, constitute the place's reason for being, in a way. It has been "improved" with them in mind. Together with some goats and a couple of horses they make it a "stock farm," a designation that usually serves to convince the mercenary outside world, including the Internal Revenue Service, that I'm not hopelessly impractical in my possession of the better part of a square mile of rough country most of which is suitable for nothing but herbivores and wild things.

Another trouble is that for foggy and complex reasons I like cows, stupid or not, and like the simple, only occasionally arduous, annual routine of working with them. Beef cattle take care of themselves during a good part of a normal year if given enough pasture to graze—what constitutes "enough"

78

varying quite a bit from region to region. In my neighborhood the carrying capacity of average unimproved grassland is usually stated as about twenty acres per animal unit: i.e., one grown cow with or without a calf, or equivalent numbers or fractions of other beasts depending on size and appetite. Elsewhere the requisite acreage may be considerably less or a great deal more, according to rainfall and the richness of the land. Whatever it is, if you stay within it, most years your cattle will be all right with only a little labor on your part. If you don't you'll run out of grass, have to buy and haul in a lot of feed, and get to watch your denuded topsoil escape as silt or dust under rains and winds, but of course you'll be in good historic company. Overstocking has long been the rule in most of the West and elsewhere, and it still is among some operators. Of one rancher in Bosque County just south of me, they used to say that every morning he'd go to a slope in his pasture and lie down on his belly, and if by looking up toward the hilltop and the sky he could see a sprig of anything growing, he'd go out and buy another ten cows.

Much of the work with cattle lies in making sure they've got enough to eat during the hard parts of the year, chiefly winter, and that what they eat has all they need in it. This means storing up hay in spring and summer for the dead months and hauling it to them in a pickup when needed, sowing wheat or oats or rye on patches of arable land in fall for green high-protein grazing while regular grasses are dormant, and buying supplements and processed feed for use when rains fail or extreme cold keeps the green stuff from growing. Dry summers mean some extra feeding too. Otherwise, except for such general rancherly activities as doctoring occasional injuries and ailments, keeping an eye on first-calf heifers in case they need obstetrical help, segregating the younger ones against rape before their time, spraying or dusting the herd against flies, and fighting back brush in pastures to keep it from crowding out grass, the main work has to do with the production and nurture and management of calves, which are your stock farm's primary crop and the chief source of such cash profit, if any, as you will enjoy from it.

In the days when the horrific screw-worm was bad in Texas one of its favorite points of attack was the navels of newborn calves, where an infection could quickly prove fatal. Sensible owners therefore tried to restrict calving to winter and early spring before the flies that bred these gnawing maggots appeared—which, gestation being a little over nine months, meant running a bull with the cows from about February until midsummer and then taking him away to dwell lovelessly in solitude or with some steers or horses. Nowadays, with the problem largely eliminated by annual releases of sterile male flies along the border and in northern Mexico, some of us still more or less follow the old schedule either because we're hidebound or because we pessimistically expect the flies to bypass the control program one of these years and come down in swarms again. Others avail themselves of new freedom by arranging to calve in spring and early summer when grasses are usually lush and cows' production of milk is highest.

Most range calves manage to get born without trouble at whatever time of year, and if they have good mothers grow healthily to the age of four or five months before you need to worry much about doing anything to them, though some graziers put out creep feeders to promote growth—roofed bins full of rich stuff that the calves can reach but larger stock can't. But at some point they need to be "worked," a process which I've found sometimes inflicts a bit of trauma on visiting non-enthusiasts but which, despite a component of casual brutality, is for cowmen a rather exhilarating task that has in it not only a lot of fine dust and bellowing and kicking and uproar but also the solid satisfaction of bringing order out of chaos. The main operations are inoculation of the calves against two or three common diseases (more in humid regions), marking them with a brand and/or earmarks and/or numbered eartags, worming where intestinal worms are a problem, dehorning horned breeds if you dislike horns, and castrating the males.

Except on some big ranches and among people who just like cowboying, few calves these days are worked in the old colorful way with ropers on horseback and other people who throw the beasts and hold them down while still others utilize knives and syringes and branding irons. Skilled help in this as in other realms is short, so instead, nearly all small operators and most big ones do the job with a minimum of assistants by driving or tolling the herd into a set of pens, separating the calves, and shunting them through alleys and chutes to some device that catches them and holds them more or less firmly. This can be a simple headgate that grabs the neck or, more efficiently and expensively, a squeeze chute that clamps on the whole creature or a "calf cradle" that not only clamps but then swings up and presents him to the attentions of his nurturers like, in the poet's phrase, a patient etherized upon a table. Except that anesthesia is not a part of the process.

Anthropomorphism being what it is, castration is the part that fascinates and bothers unaccustomed spectators most, especially male ones. It needs to be done in part because the market usually pays better for steers than for bulls, though many will argue with you that there is no difference in their meat. But the chief reason for it is convenience in handling cattle. Steers are docile, they can be put into a pasture with big nubile heifers without fear the latter will be bred too young, and above all they lack the sexual smolder that sends even young bulls on patrol along fencelines, looking for a way out and often finding it.

On very young calves castration can be accomplished with practically no shock to either subject or witnesses by using a tool that places a heavy tight rubber band around the upper part of the scrotum, which subsequently atrophies and falls off. But in older animals this poses some danger of tetanus, and they have to be done with the ancient and very efficient knife or some other cutting instrument, or with bloodless emasculators like the Burdizzo, a heavy set of compound-leverage pincers that crush the spermatic cord without breaking skin. This implement was invented many years ago by an old Italian vet, whose name it bears and whom it made rich, and is still manufactured painstakingly in Milan for use throughout the world's warm regions where fresh wounds are subject to quick infection and to parasites. The instructions that come with it bear the doctor's mustached, starch-collared likeness and a rather hilarious photograph of a calf that must have been tranquilized to the gills, since he is shown submitting to the operation without a surge or a kick or, as far as can be told, a bellow of indignation. . . . Here in the Southwest the Burdizzo had its heyday when the screw-worms were having theirs, but even now a good many people, myself among them, still like it for its cleanness and lessened shock effect, though it's more trouble than a knife and can hardly be called humane.

Having worked your calves, the main thing you do with them is sell them at weaning age, six months or so, or maybe a bit earlier or later according to rises and falls in the market and the state of your own pastures for sustaining some extra eaters over a period of time. After perhaps setting aside a steer to keep for fattening and slaughter and a few good heifers to raise as replacements for cows that need to be culled, you load the rest of the calves into a trailer and haul them to a weekly auction at some county seat not far away or maybe, if prices are rumored to be better there, to a city sale like the one on Fort Worth's North Side.

To confess a weakness, I find culling cows harder than almost anything to do with cattle except the worst kind of bloody obstetrics. With a small herd you come to know your animals as individuals and even if you don't view them sentimentally you have favorites among them and a relationship with the whole bunch based on what they have done for you and the longstanding responsibility you've exercised toward them. Hence it weighs a bit on the conscience when one of them has to go the hamburger route, which is where most cull cows do go, because she's started having sorry calves or no calves at all, and it weighs still more when drouth or a hard winter strikes, or cash is requisite, or the herd simply grows too large for the land you've got, and you have to cut back by selling several and need to decide which ones. Records help if you keep them, scribbled notebook pages that detail cows' lineage, birth, quirks, achievements, and imperfections, much in the manner of military service record books or a nosy government's dossiers on its citizens. If, for instance, a bright, large-eyed, trusting, shapely little cow named Pet, who will take feed cubes from your hand and will suffer her ears to be scratched, has been producing tiny calves that never get very big and are prone to things like warts, and an ill-tempered, ungainly, suspicious creature known only as Number Thirty-nine has been rearing one after another a succession of large, thrifty sons and daughters, the records will show it and you know what you have to do. Pet goes, even if the innocent confusion you think to read in her face, as she's hustled through the ring to the music of cracking whips and shouts and the auctioneer's amplified gabble, does cause twinges in your breast.

Not that cold reason always prevails, even with tougher

types than me. I once saw an ancient scrub brindle rack of bones, with one horn up and the other down, in the sleek Beefmaster herd of a rancher reputed to be hardnosed and practical, and asked what she was doing there.

"Oh, Rosie," he said with a shake of his grizzled head, evading the question. "Seventeen years old."

"But why?"

"Guess I like her," he answered with finality and I did not press, for it is unwise to tread on hard people's softnesses.

There are lots of us miniature ranchers across the continent. The scorn expressed by that expert Aggie and by others like him is not at all disinterested but sprouts, I think, from an uneasiness that afflicts agri-bigness types when they're brought eyeball to eyeball with the fact that a goodly percentage of the cattle marketed in the nation these days comes out of small to middlesized herds more or less like mine. This uneasiness afflicts others too, including old-line ranchers, who rather bitterly circulate among themselves such statistical gems as the one that ninety percent of the cattle in the fabulous feedlots of the Texas Panhandle come from the herds of people who own ten cows or less. That figure is hostile hyperbole, but the real ones are impressive enough. A Texas agricultural census shows that in 1974 people with fewer than fifty calving beef cows owned eighteen percent of well over five million such cows in the state, and people with fewer than one hundred cows—still relative small-timers in economic terms—owned thirty-eight percent.

What probably bothers our friend the Aggie most is that we're unpredictable, that the unexpectedly large or small numbers of beasts that whim or panic causes us to trailer to sales from year to year are a large factor in the market and can mean the loss or gain of millions by feedlots and commodity speculators and other would-be beneficiaries, according to whether they have second-guessed us well or badly. And what understandably gravels real ranchers is that after decades of hardship based on generally poor cattle prices, inflation, rising land and inheritance taxes, and whatnot, they are losing much of what little control they had over their own product to a rabble of johnny-come-latelies. This irritation is heightened by a deterioration of old ranching standards, especially a loss of prestige by the stalwart British breeds of cattle and a new demand for crossbred stuff which is favored by the feedlots, and therefore by the whole market, because its "hybrid vigor" enables it to gain weight faster at less cost— even if, as some ranchers claim and I tend to believe, the meat is not quite so good.

"People like you are just messing things up," one rancher said amiably to me a few years back, when the dimensions of all this were growing visible. His ancestral land was measured in quite a few square-mile sections instead of acres and stocked with several hundred big handsome whitefaces whose careful improvement, through selective breeding and the introduction of bulls from new bloodlines, had begun in his grandfather's time. "You can't make a living out of a little herd like that, and nothing that you do with them is ever done quite right. But there are so damn many of you that you're interfering with the way things are supposed to be. The other day I shipped a truckload of nice prime calves to Fort Worth, and I got six or eight cents a pound less for them than the buyers were bidding for little bunches of raunchy speckled stuff raised by weekend amateurs in the Blacklands and East Texas and Arkansas and God knows where else."

"I've got Angus," I said a bit defensively. "I didn't invent hybrid vigor either."

"Scrub vigor," he said with contempt. But the last time I saw him, a year or so ago, he spoke with enthusiasm about the crossbred calves he was getting from running Charolais bulls with his Hereford cows. Things change, and on the list of proud traditional ranching's troubles we stock-farm types are only a single item—another and more hurtful one being agribusiness itself and the sophisticated activities of "cattle-men" more at home with pocket calculators than saddles and with steer-futures hedging than the identification of range grasses.

There is nothing new about owning a few beef cows, especially in places like Texas where social cachet of a sort has always attached to their possession and the ability to jaw about them. But the emergence of smallish grazing operations as a major sort of land use, from the upper-middle Atlantic coast down through and across the South and in parts of the Midwest as well, has taken place mainly since World War II, I believe, for various reasons of which the strongest are not social and may not even be economic. In part it grew out of the agricultural desolation of the Thirties, when farming was a dead end, and out of government emphasis since that time on taking marginal and tired or wornout country out of cultivation and sowing it to improved permanent grasses to let it rest and to stop erosion. In high-rainfall areas with deep soil, properly managed and fertilized grassland of this sort can be astoundingly productive of beef. Not uncommonly it will sustain a cow on every two or three acres or so, though in time, as world hunger swells, most places with such potential will likely be put back into crops. In less rich terrain, including places like my beat-up patch of rocky hills, the land's carrying capacity is skimpier, but on the other hand grazing is about all it's good for these days anyhow.

One element in beef cattle's appeal is the fact, already in-timated, that they represent a lot less work than farming or horticulture, taking care of their own needs much of the time if given half a chance. This has weight with many owners who want their land to pay its way, but who make their main living in towns and cities, and on weekends either don't have time for agriculture or possess an immunity to the sentimental pull of plow and harrow. During market upsurges cattle can also bring in a fair amount of money, and such is human nature that upsurge prices are what cattlemen like to view as the norm, just as farmers are in love with the boom-based reference point of "parity." We are still in an upsurge just now, but unfortunately these joyous intervals have seldom lasted long, for when they begin large numbers of erstwhile spectators jump in, buy overpriced breeding stock of whatever description with borrowed money, throw them onto leased pasture, and flood the market with calves as promptly as biology permits, driving prices back down again. Thus a sleek, staggering, moony-eyed, newborn bullcalf, which your doting mind's eye sees as being worth, say, three hundred dollars or more as a weaned steer a few months later, may turn out to bring half that sum, a crucial difference considering steady inflation and the feed and hay and other things you will have invested in his mama during the long months of pregnancy and nursing. Sad to say, hardship ensues, whether small-scale or large and whether to high flyers or to the rest of us.

Nothing illustrates better the main reason, the irrational one, for the nineteen-cow phenomenon than the fact that so many of us stay with cattle despite such setbacks. We like the damned things, and our real motivation has little to do with money or labor but I suppose must be called romantic. Possibly the pull of the legendary Old West has something to do with it, for in the arteries of the purest romantics among us cowboy blood pumps hot and strong. Big hats and sharp-toed boots are common attire in regions where forty years ago their wearers would have been laughed back into brogans and farmer-style caps, and on full many a hundred-and-sixty-acre spread, on Saturdays, lariats of nylon hiss through the air and traildrivers born too late for the trail whoop yee-haw as they pound along on horseback behind high-tailed fleeing kine, making them wild as deer.

But the majority of us, Old Westerners at heart or no, do things with less flamboyance, mainly because this is easier on both the cattle and us. Some are highly progressive and thoughtful about the matter of management, perhaps lately graduated from some evening-college course in animal husbandry and loaded with data on the protein content of various feeds, artificial insemination, calf "gainability," and pregnancy testing. Others, maybe most, have read a few books and watched the way other folks do things and get along on that, and still others cling to casual methods, right or wrong, picked up in rural youth. A few happy-go-luckies engage in hardly any management at all, letting the beasts run nearly wild within their boundary fences to multiply or die and every once in a while, by one means or another, gathering up calves and selling them. And another contingent, gamblers at heart, keep no breeding stock but buy steers and heifers small and sell them large, at a profit if they're lucky.

Thus, clearly, unless a nineteen-cowman's proclivities get him slantwise with some local SPCA chapter or cause him to lose so much money that he goes broke, there is wide flexibility as to how much he needs to know and what he does with his cattle. There is also a rich variety of breeds from which he may choose—the old Herefords and Shorthorns and Anguses, Brahmans and genetically stabilized Brahman crosses like Branguses and Santa Gertrudis and Beefmasters, modish newer "exotics" such as Charolais and Simmentals and Chianinas and Limousins, and quite a few other sorts ranging from Devons and Highlands to tiny Dexters. And in a day when "hybrid vigor" is a magic phrase, unstabilized crosses of every sort abound, whether planned with care by breeders who know what they're after in terms of shape and size, or achieved less studiously by someone who just dumps a bunch of varied cows into a pasture with some sort of bull and occasionally comes up with results that would appear to have been flown in by jet cargo plane from Masai-land. The ancient and tough and wily Longhorn has its partisans, and some owners even edge away from the genus *Bos* into things like buffaloes and Beefaloes and exotic game animals. And each and every kind of creature that I've named and a good many that I haven't possess distinctive qualities of physique and psyche which some human beings will admire and swear by and others will just swear at.

Small-scale beginners are often advised that they will do best to specialize in costly purebred registered beasts of whatever ilk, since the calves will be salable at premium prices, as heifers or bulls, to other breeders—who, the theory implies, will come flocking around checkbook in hand without even being asked. This can be true enough in time if the beginner in question knows or quickly learns a good bit about genetics and conformation and artificial insemination and such things, maybe wins some prizes at livestock shows to build his herd's reputation, and builds his own by scrupulous attention to records and frank dealing with buyers. But not all of us are that fond of intricate record keeping, fuss and feathers, and the very special perfectionism and politics of the show ring, and there are some other difficulties with purebreds as well, especially in the rough country where some of us run our herds. Living on one end of your place you often find it hard to know precisely what's going on at the other ends, and hard also to keep fences in perfect repair at places where they cross streams and gullies. One visit from a neighbor's offbreed bull can wreck a purebred operation's purity for a year and reduce the calf crop's value to whatever a country auction ring determines it to be, and the young bulls you're keeping for sale to those eager buyers can wander too, messing up lineage records.

Hence registered stock is not for everyone, and most of us settle for something less expensive and less prestigious like my "grade" Anguses, maybe keeping purebred bulls with them year after year so that quality steadily improves even if pedigree doesn't. We find them good to look at, though increasingly with time we are nagged by an impulse to get a bull of another color and produce some of those bouncing, hybridly vigorous mongrels that consistently bring up to a dime or fifteen cents a pound more at sales than good calves of straight British breed. Even if we don't like their looks . . .

Having made a little money on cattle in certain years and lost some of it back in others, having worried over an uneconomic small herd through drouths and bad winters with an intensity that would have been more wisely saved for life's main problems, having been kicked, butted, stomped, and run up corral fences countless times by Number Thirty-nine and others of like temperament, having pounded large quantities of time down a rat hole over the years in the maintenance of this grudging place for bovine use, and having liked just about all of it at least in retrospect, I am still fond of cows and of tending them and am sometimes puzzled, along with other devotees, to find that everyone everywhere doesn't feel the same way. My original eight heifers have all now gone down the long trail to McDonald's, the last of them just this year at a quite advanced age, but I remember them well by looks and traits and names—Roy's Mother, Nutty Johnson, White Tits, Big Navel, and the others—and take simpleminded pleasure in recognizing among members of the present group some cast of eye, some set of neck, some belligerence or timidity, some tone of bellow that traces back to one of those founding mothers.

I can't even work up any shame about the fact that such

things matter to me, nor do I really much care what it was that caused them to matter to me in the first place, whether the romance of the West, or osmotic absorption in youth of the basic Texas myth of ranches and ranching, or a memory derived from the collective unconscious of some Neolithic herding time when human life was pretty carefree. And while I still may manage to break loose from cows one of these years, I know already that if I do I won't regret having expended time and energy on them. Because it seems they are something I needed to know about, and in a day when knowledge that you don't need comes washing in on your brain in waves like surf, it is good to have a little that you do.

I'm not talking about practical needs, any more than most other cow people are even when they think otherwise. Few of them, at any rate, have trouble in getting the point of an aged joke, maybe Neolithic itself, that is reshaped and recirculated from time to time. In one version it tells of a leathery West Texan who has fought all his life for a minimal living on a few sections of caliche and stones, but has now been blessed with a couple of million dollars of unexpected oil money. When queried as to what he intends to do he reflects for a moment and says, "No, I ain't heading for Las Vegas and all them naked floozies. I ain't going to buy me no Cadillacs either. I figure to do something different."

"You do?" say his questioners.

"Hell, yes," he says. "What I figure to do is just ranch and ranch and ranch and ranch, till every damn last cent of that money is all used up."

A Few Words
in Favor of Goats

Goats undoubtedly matter to more people in the world than Texans do, but in general Texans themselves don't know or care much about goats. It is possible to consider this peculiar, in light of a couple of facts. First, the state can be regarded in one sense as a sort of northern outpost or cutting edge of Latin-American civilization, and Latins, whether on home ground along the Mediterranean or over here, are among the world's goat experts par excellence. But all that this lore boils down to for most Texans, including I fear most modern Texas Latins, is an occasional expensive restaurant encounter with suckling kid, known as cabrito, and maybe a remembrance of the good stout fibrous goat cheese, pale in hue, that used to give enchiladas and chiles rellenos their whang, seldom seen now that even Mexican cooks have gone down the primrose lane with Kraft.

Furthermore we Texans have within our boundaries, or had until just lately, one of the world's great concentrations of goats in the big herds of longhaired Angoras that thrived on the liveoak and other hardwood scrub of the Edwards Plateau and similar limestone regions. But despite their numbers—over four million strong at their peak in the Sixties—I suppose the Angoras were never a big part of most Texans' consciousness, restricted as they were to some fairly lonesome parts of the state and usually hidden from the eyes of motorists by the brush in which they browsed. More than once, when traveling with city friends, I've heard them referred to as sheep. The herds shrank hugely—most were shipped to Mexico for meat—when mohair fell out of fashion and the market collapsed. And though mohair's vogue and its price have lately come back strong, ranchers' caution about further fluctuation as well as about other factors such as predation, chiefly by coyotes and dogs and hybrids thereof, has kept hair goats from regaining their old status. Much of the world's mohair is now produced by South Africa, and when you see goats on the Plateau and roundabout, they're just about as likely to be of the tough, unhairy, common sort known as "Spanish."

Both kinds control brush and furnish kids for barbecue, and both are the subject of a considerable body of ranchers' folklore involving mainly their ability to get out of where you put them into places where they're not supposed to be, such as grainfields and neighbors' pastures and highway median strips. If you want an adequate goat fence, one story goes, you build it as tight as you can with close-spaced posts and lots of upright stays and all dips in the ground beneath the wire filled with rocks or stumps or something; then you wait for a big rain and if the fence holds water it will hold your goats. Another tale describes a scientific experiment conducted at Texas A. & M. wherein three goats were stuffed into a steel drum which was then welded shut. When it was opened a week later, one goat was dead, another had screwworms, and the third one was missing.

When we used to keep a good-sized herd of Spanish goats here on our place, a few of each year's crop of weanling kids, newly independent and capable of squeezing through holes impassable to their parents, would form a teenage gang that ravaged the neighborhood. Since they usually came back and there isn't too much to ravage in these rocky hills, problems resulted only when they tried to return home through a part of the fence that had no holes in it, or when they got far enough afield to discover somebody's yard shrubbery or vegetable garden. The resultant telephone calls—beginning most often with "Are you missing any goats?"—were not invariably friendly in tone.

Sometimes the tales and the folklore have to do with goats' horrible susceptibility to predation, and most are not very funny. An early traumatic episode in my administration of this place came one January when, inspired by experimentalism and ignorance, I elected to leave forty or so Spanish goats in a rough hill pasture to kid. The foraging nannies would stash their dozing toddlers in high grass as deer do fawns, but fawns stay in place very quietly till their mothers come back whereas the newborn kids, waking hungry alone or in their twinned pairs, would begin to shrill and squeak and would bring on themselves the rapt attention of furred gourmets of various species. By the time I and my wife and a helpful neighbor had gathered up such little ones as we could find and had hustled them with the mamas and the berefts and the still-pregnants back to the house pasture, nineteen kids were left out of perhaps thirty-five that had greeted life in the past few days. Nor had I managed to find and wreak vengeance on one single member of the opposition. All I found in my armed wanderings were a few bobcat and big coon tracks and some small bloody ragged remains, when the buzzards hadn't beaten me to them. The appreciation of cabrito is widespread.

A generation or so ago in harder but more easygoing times, goats were known and taken for granted by a good many more Texans, and for that matter Americans, than know anything about them today. They existed even in cities, sheltered by crusty codgers in backyard sheds and sometimes tethered during the day in vacant lots or out among roadside weeds. Scrub milk nannies for the most part, with an occasional aromatic billy kept for propagation, they soothed many an aging or unquiet stomach with the rich liquid from their udders, furnished rolypoly manure for garden compost and kids for delicate meat, gave jesters a focus for worn boffo humor concerning tin cans and old innertubes and grateful tumblebugs, and developed evil tempers under the teasing of small boys, including me. Without ever being what you might call chic or even reputable, they hung on.

But affluence is even harder on goats than it is on human picturesqueness, and in the unreal, increasingly homogeneous glitter-island of time that urban Americans have lately been inhabiting, there is not much place for subsistence livestock, which is what goats fundamentally are. Public opinion and the public nuisance laws that reflect it have turned against them and other such creatures, and you usually have to go out beyond a city's limits to its unzoned, often unincorporated fringes to find any goats at all, and not many even there. Milk comes less arduously though not cheaper in cartons, and there has been among us a dwindling of stubborn country-bred old folks who cling to subsistence ways. If city vegetable gardening, based on poison-fear and anger at market prices and quality, is on the boom these days, city goat-keeping has not been following suit.

Farther from cities, though, goats are in pretty good shape, and I'm not talking about big ranch herds. How much of the new population trend away from metropolitan centers, confirmed by the Census Bureau, represents flight to a less hectic but still supermarket-centered existence in small towns or exurban "developments," and how much consists of neo-homesteaders moving whole or part hog back to the land to live and subsist, I have no way of knowing. But in a time like ours when many view the urban future quite dimly, there are notable numbers of these latter from young to medium-old in vintage, searching out their destined two or ten or twenty or more acres, building a home or refurbishing an old one, laying out gardens and orchards, learning to grind wheat and corn for bread and maybe to ferment their own beer and wine, training and preparing for tough times if they come. Some have the cash to pay for all this out of pocket; others manage by commuting back to good jobs in the cities they have left, or otherwise.

As often as not their plans include livestock, preferably in small numbers and not too daunting in size. If they have in mind producing their own milk and butter and cheese, goats are made to order for them. Hence in the past few years there has been a solid little boom in the breeding and sale of pedigreed dairy goats and a rocketing of their value. Breeders of good reputation with some show champions in their herds are asking and getting up to four or five hundred dollars for four-month-old weaned doe kids—"doe" and "buck" in this more genteel goat world having supplanted the old vacant-lot terms "nanny" and "billy." Americans like to go first class, and these goats definitely do have chic, at least in given circles.

If they're willing to pay that much for a young beast that

won't be productive for another year or so, as much as a first-rate milk cow would cost, the clear inference is that they most specifically want a goat. It was not always so in rural America. The traditional American family farm, the sort of holding people went to the frontier to stake out for themselves until the frontier reached country too dry to sustain traditional farm life, had little use for goats but relied instead on cows of which the classic types were the big-eyed sweet-breathed Jerseys and Guernseys and Ayrshires beloved of children's-book illustrators. There were some reasons for this. For one thing, most of those farmers' ancestry traced back to the British lowlands and north Europe where cow's-milk cultures prevailed. Another reason was great big families—you need a fair group of people and a couple of pigs besides to do justice to the three daily gallons or so that a good milk cow can yield. And still another was the prime land that characterizes, or did before old-style agriculture chewed the topsoil from so much of it, farms in the eastern United States. For the milk cow is a good-land animal, faring and producing but poorly in deserts and semi-deserts and mountains and the earth's other reaches of marginal and submarginal soil, whether shaped by climate or man's abuse or both.

Those reaches are the true stomping ground of the goat, which can climb nearly anywhere and thrive on skimpy forage in places that would starve a cow or a sheep. The names of the best-known breeds mirror such origins—Toggenburg and Saanen (both Swiss to start with), Alpine, Murcian (named after an Iberian province and the rootstock of most of the hardy "Spanish" goats of Mexico and South Texas), Nubian, even Angora for that matter. . . . The Scottish Highlands cherished goats, and so did Norway, the vast high arid places of Asia, the rocky parts of Ireland, and the lands along the Mediterranean after the ancients had worn them out. A well-established slander, which still crops up in forums like the

U.N., holds goats responsible for much of the ecological devastation in such places. This is resented aloud or in published form by goat people, including such luminaries as the late Scottish expert David Mackenzie, whose wise and whimsical *Goat Husbandry* remains in print as a sort of Bible for the whole clan. There is no question that goats out of control can do big damage, as they have on many small islands without predators, where breeding stock was turned loose two hundred or more years ago by ships from maritime nations to furnish meat for future voyagers—R. Crusoe and his real-life prototype Alexander Selkirk having been beneficiaries of that practice. But in an area like the Mediterranean basin, for instance, the indictment is flimsy. Man with his reckless hillside farming, his vast herds of any and all species of livestock, his axes and saws and ever-waxing numbers—man is the one who did it. And if goats are still around consolidating the damage because they're the only domesticated beasts that can now survive in some parts of the region, that is hardly the goats' own fault.

Goats also spread long ago, though never thickly, to many richer regions. The root cause was socio-economic, not unlike that which sprinkled scrub nannies about the cities of my youth. If you have a held-down peasantry shut off from ownership of good land and restricted in terms of livestock to creatures that can be kept in a dooryard or pastured alongside roads or on moors and other waste places, you have a ready-made body of goat enthusiasts. The link with such owners did little for goats' social standing, of course, and in most north-European countries they were and remain somewhat grubby figures of fun. Which makes it all the more remarkable that upperclass Britishers of the past century or so, with the pleasant unmercenary thrust toward investigation and discovery and perfecting things that so many of that ilk have possessed, have had much to do with firming up the main breeds of dairy goats and improving them into the beautifully efficient milk producers they are today. And in this country, people far different from the crusty backyard codgers of yesteryear have carried on with the refinement process.

If the neo-homesteaders who inherit the results continue to increase or merely manage to hang on at their present level, it seems likely that goats will keep on having a place among us too. It is not just small holdings and small families that make them popular among such people, nor is it just each doe's daily gallon or so of rich sweet milk, far different from the strong stuff many of us recall getting with our morning *café con leche* during sojourns in rural Mexico, where billies run free with the herds and their stink gets into everyone and everything. In large measure it's also the potent charm that nearly all goats have, and the variations in personality that are as sharp as in dogs and cats. They play among themselves, and to see a file of them dancing and bucking sideways in sheer pleasure as they head for pasture in the morning is to know why our words "caper" and "caprice" come from the Latin for goat. They play with people too, and nuzzle and demand and talk, and most people who know them talk back. Call it sentimentality if you like, but I have known some very hardeyed types, with no soft feelings otherwise discernible, who habitually conversed with goats. Goats are gentle beings by nature and for every one that butts people there is a corresponding human, nearly always young and male, who helped to develop the habit. They deserve to survive, and people will survive a bit more richly if they have some goats around.

I'll confess that the milk sort are a lot of trouble unless your life's pattern jibes well with their ways. Twice a day with feed and bucket you have to *be* there, not in Austin or Fort Worth or a few miles away sipping beer and swapping goat folklore with some friends. Your failure to show up when the established, precise, magical hour for milking rolls around will mean that when you do come home you'll have to face a very disgruntled and loudmouthed set of goats, and if you do it often their disgust will evince itself in very measly production. Here at the place, for such reasons, we reluctantly sold all our best milk goats last year and at present have only one old pet Nubian, now dry, and a handful of Spanish goats that come to the corral at night for a ration of corn and protection against coyotes and roving dogs. Even these half-wild specimens have stout individualities and names, and my younger daughter can usually trace the ancestry of any kid in the bunch from Doorbell down through William and Creampuff and Pearlie May or whoever, which can make for problems at barbecue time.

As for the hand-raised lactating pets we got rid of last year, it turns out in a way that we didn't. When driving past the ranch where they now live, as pampered as ever, I find myself being forced by my females, and sometimes when alone by inner compulsion, to drop in and see them and be greeted with recognition and old affection. I never specifically visited a cow in my life, or a horse, or a dog except at the vet's. But I seem to visit goats.

Of Bees and Men

People who've had occasion to get to know honeybees tend to develop strong feelings about them, though such occasions are growing rarer in a mainly urban world. As often as not the feelings come out as aversion, because a bee can sting and where there's one there are generally thousands more, all with the same capability. The other members of my own family, all female, are pretty much of this persuasion as are the dogs and most other resident mammalian friends, so that when I am working—or playing, or whatever it is—in the little apiary beside the garden, with veil affixed to head and smoker stuffed with smoldering burlap or cow chips, I can count on being left severely alone. My ladies do like what the bees produce, however, and are skilled at uncapping combs with a hot knife and spinning them in the old-fashioned crank extractor and straining and bottling the honey during the various pleasant times of harvest that come in spring and summer.

A good many other people—I guess it will be taken as chauvinistic if I say they are mostly male, but for whatever reason this is so—are from the time of their first experience with bees seized by fascination with them, as I was in my turn. Time and again I've seen it happen here at the place, especially in April and May on pretty weekends when friends drive out from the cities to visit and my hives, freed from the winter's long torpor and swollen with newborn workers, are likely to be in a swarming mood. A roar starts in the bee yard and a swirling tower of frantic, happy, golden bugs evolves in the air above it, to settle finally with their queen in a fat cluster dangling from some nearby limb, from which way-station they will send out scouts to find a new abode. It is an exhilarating and somehow awesome sight for old hands and neophytes alike, though the beekeeper's own enjoyment of it may be tempered with mild disgust at the fact that his early-spring manipulations in the hives, designed to prevent such divisions and thus to increase his take of honey, have yet once more been bilked by the bees' overriding instinct to be fruitful and multiply and spread themselves through the world.

But having failed in that, he needs at any rate to catch the swarm and start another hive with it. So he fetches his paraphernalia—a new hive box with frames and wax comb foundation, a saw or pruning shears, a ladder and catch bag maybe if the swarm is high—and dons a veil and fires up a smoker. And at about that point, nearly always, certain of the visiting friends start wanting to know if there are extra veils for them. There are, so they take part in the whole business with him, helping or hindering but with dogged interest sticking to the end even if he bungles and, as I did once last spring, manages to drop the sawed-off limb with the swarm while descending his ladder and creates large-scale angry uproar. Swarming bees are gentle creatures, full of honey and looking for a home, but no bees stay gentle if mishandled. . . . At any rate, after he has finally gotten them to the new hive, shaken them in, smoked them down among the frames, and squatted there for a while watching to make certain he has caught the queen and they are going to stay, the friends start asking questions. Unsure of what they've seen, they're convinced it was worth seeing and they want to know as much about it as you can tell them.

Yes, there was another queen left behind in the old colony, which will regain its strength again by fall. No, you can't put the swarm back where it came from, not without more elaborate and skilled machinations than a hacker like me wants to fool with. Yes, it's a nice big bunch of bees, maybe eight or ten pounds, but because of the effort it will need to expend building comb and rearing new generations of workers, it probably won't make more than just enough honey this summer to get itself through next winter, which is after all the bees' main purpose that we seek to pervert into surplus production for our own greedy use. Yes, no, maybe . . . And as the questions continue I know quite certainly that a couple of new beekeepers have been created, if they ever get a place where they can set up a few hives of their own.

But with opportunities for such conversion getting scarcer, I suppose that on the whole public opinion in relation to our ancient small friend the honeybee is rather queasy, especially since widespread ignorance causes said small friend to get blamed for many stings inflicted by wasps and other ill-natured hymenoptera. The media, for which alarm and threat are the fodder of daily function, have much to do with this. Bees equal stings equal copy. Hence the uncertain march of Brazilian-African "killer bees" up the Isthmus and toward our own tender skins is always good for a little horrified conversation when sex and football and politics pall, and no spring is complete without newspaper and TV coverage of two or three or more swarms of bees that have clustered on unlikely objects such as traffic lights or motorcycle handlebars or baseball backstops. The beekeeper who is called in by the authorities to take the swarm away is inevitably hailed as a Saint George rescuing the public from a menace. If before his arrival the public in question has perpetrated some of the common idiocies like swatting the swarm with poles or pelting it with stones or squirting it with water or fly spray, old Saint George may deserve a bit of acclaim, for a menace has indeed been created and people have been getting stung, as George himself will be too before he manages to stuff his several thousand enraged bees into a box or a bag. But most often he does the job swiftly and easily and safely and ends up with the esteem of his fellow men plus maybe thirty or forty or fifty dollars worth of insects, at current package-bee prices, for very little labor.

When people lived mainly in the country and in small towns, more of them had an easy, friendly familiarity with bees and their habits, based not only on the presence of hives in back gardens and alongside fields and roads but also on the very old practice, shared by man with bears and other sweet-prone beasts, of robbing wild colonies of their accumulated hoard of honey, and in primitive times and places of their tender young grubs as well, the latter being a protein-rich snack that has somehow lost favor in our time. On the wall of a rock-shelter in eastern Spain, archaeologists found a painting, dating by one estimate from 15,000 B.C., which shows men with ropes and baskets inflicting such larceny on a colony ensconced in a hole in a cliff. The bees are depicted as very large and excited and the human thieves are undoubtedly getting hell stung out of them, but insofar as the graceful sketch allows one to judge they seem happy at their work.

As well they may have been. Honey is the only concentrated sweet that can be used in its natural form without processing, and it was the only concentrated sweet that Europeans knew at all before the advent, at some point in the so-called Dark Ages, of sugar, which for a number of centuries thereafter was a scarce and costly item. Honey was the old sweet, the real sweet that men have always known.

At an uncertain but very early date, people learned enough about bees' ways to start keeping them in hollow logs and inverted pots and baskets and other such receptacles, and a passion for honey extended itself into a respect and often a reverence for the wee beasties who knew how to make it. By the time of the First Dynasty in Egypt, around 3000 B.C., beekeeping had taken on a bit of sophistication and involved such practices as floating large numbers of stacked clay tube-hives up and down the Nile on rafts to take advantage of the bloom of nectar-producing flowers here and there, and the Pharaohs appropriated the sign of the bee as a personal symbol. Assyrian notables' corpses were painted with beeswax and submerged in honey for entombment; the Old Testament holds pleasant references to apicultural products ("My son," said the Solomon of Proverbs, "eat thou honey, because it is good; and the honeycomb which is sweet to thy taste . . ."); and few nature-minded thinkers of note in classic times, from Democritus and Aristotle down through Virgil and Columella and Pliny, failed to pay their respects to *Apis mellifera* and to add to the store of information and misinformation that was piling up. Medieval monks advanced the art a bit, and in more recent centuries a series of discoveries by bright men who got themselves hooked on bees, like me and my April friends, led to the more or less scientific management prevalent today.

This management has little to do with the "domestication" of bees, which remain essentially wild creatures capable of surviving on their own, even though particularly gentle or productive strains have been identified—even bred—and then promoted and spread around. What it mainly consists of is a set of techniques for guiding their complex wild instincts toward greater usefulness—techniques of hiving and adding or subtracting space and manipulating colonies for their own wellbeing and for a bigger yield of honey. It is, of course, still possible to keep them in the old ways that date back forever, and for a non-scientific type like me there is sometimes a temptation to do so when modern methods gang agley and fail of their main purpose. An old man who died here in our cedar hills three or four years ago maintained dozens of colonies in gutted TV cabinets and surplus ammunition boxes and cracked Styrofoam ice chests and whatnot, worried very minimally about them, and got a lot of honey too.

As Old World men spread over the globe they took their sweet tooth and their Old World bees along with them, often supplanting native species like the tropical American stingless bees, whose honey and wax had been demanded as tribute from conquered jungle tribes by the Incas long before Columbus. New England settlers brought honeybees, as did Virginians and others, and the Spanish are said to have introduced them into Mexico and our present Southwest. The bees took it from there, dispersing into the wilds as escaped swarms and moving so far ahead of the white frontier that they became a part of untamed Indians' lore and way of life as well. Here in Texas, for instance, the main southern band of Comanches, by the time history took much note of them, had assumed the name of Honey-eaters. They didn't take on sweetness of nature with it, though. Like moderns who get their honey in supermarkets, they were willing enough to let others take their stings for them; one account exists of naked

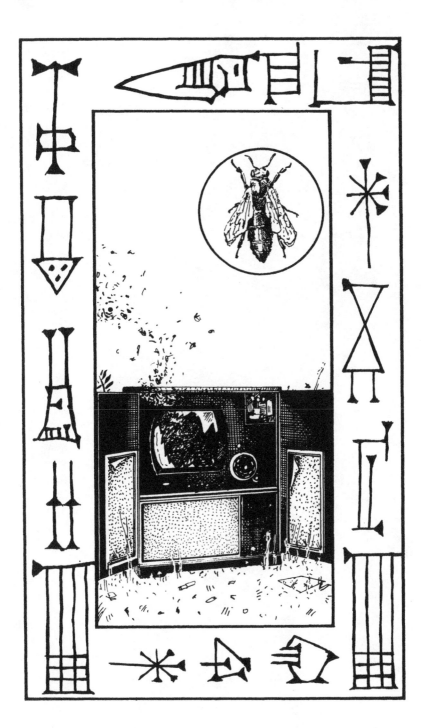

white captives being dangled on lariats by such Comanches down a cliff face to rob a hive in a crevice, much in the manner of those immortalized Mesolithic Valencians, except that the captives don't appear to have been very happy about the whole thing.

But I would not want to dwell overmuch on stings. If you duff around with bees the fact is you get stung a little and sometimes more than that, but nearly always through your own awkwardness or haste or because out of pigheadedness or necessity you go into the hives on a chilly or wet day when the workers are all at home and waiting around for something to resent. In good times, say during the May–June flow of nectar from the sweetclover that we often sow in fall among the winter grain, the bees at their work pay you little mind and you can play with them and study their growing larvae and the buildup of honey for days on end without a single sting. Nor with time do the stings seem to matter as much; you take those that come with relative calm, not only because you've learned that jerking about and swatting merely lead to more stings but also because, unless you're one of the rare hypersensitive types, you've developed a sort of immunity to them. It always hurts when a bee prongs you hard, but you stop swelling and itching afterward. One old hawknosed fellow I knew long ago used to work his crude box hives quite ungently without a veil and with only a burning roll of old quilt for a smoker, hacking out full honeycombs with a butcherknife, and when he got through, that great beak of his, that veritable prow, would be so stuck full of stings it looked furry, but it never turned red or enlarged. His eyes didn't even water.

For that matter a reasonable amount of stinging may be good for you. In reinforcement of what has been observed for centuries among elderly apiarists, some quite respectable medical authorities think bee venom helps to prevent and alleviate certain forms of arthritis. Others say good honey will help the same affliction, and once it was used as an effective antiseptic for wounds, since germs do very poorly in it. In recent years an Oklahoma allergist has made a case for pure and unprocessed honey—not subjected to heat and only coarsely strained, unlike the pretty commercial stuff—as a cure for much hay fever and asthma. Suspended pollen does the trick, apparently, and I believe the recommendation is that the honey be taken from bees working within fifteen miles or so of where the sufferer lives and that it be swallowed in small quantities each day. Unfortunately for a good many of us it has no effect on allergies to things like carpet-mold and dog hair that do not interest bees, or our Texas juniper whose pollen permeates the air in winter while sensible bees are holed up sucking on last summer's honey.

Bees open your eyes to all sorts of matters around you—to weather and winds and soil moisture that affect the prospects for nectar, to creatures like toads and tanagers and skunks and dragonflies and wax moths that prey on your hives in one fashion or another, though seldom to the point that they have to be fought off. But most of all to plants, to the multitudinous species of wildflowers and blossoming trees and shrubs that bees work during the week or two of their glory, and to those more useful blooms of wild or seeded things (here where I am, mainly sweetclover and vetch and mesquite and sumac, and maybe a few miles off a completely different array) that last for five or six weeks and in good moist seasons provide a "honey flow" for your aggrandizement and the hives'. Or sometimes for theirs alone, as with broomweed, which makes an unpleasant dark honey smelling faintly of dirty socks but, flowering as it does copiously in fall, packs the hives with fuel against winter.

As students of plant life, beekeepers tend more toward pragmatism than toward scientific detachment. An occasional misfit gets led astray into esthetic or purely botanical realms of interest; not being wholly practical myself I have sinned a bit in that direction. But your real hard-line dedicated apiarist focuses his considerable powers of discernment on a restricted field of botany, specifically on nectar-yielding flora within a mile of wherever he has a set of hives, which is about as far as he can expect his bees to wander foraging. He distinguishes among plants too, according to the flavor of the honey they yield, and takes a dim view of things like prickly ash, broom-weed, and privet, whose product is unpalatable to most human tongues. Such a man's eyes miss very few flowering things and he is full of information if you can get it out of him. But a rare orchid from the jungles of Darien could sprout miraculously some morning on one of his pasture oaks, and unless bees were sipping its fluids his gaze would very likely pass along else-where.

All is not well with beekeeping nowadays. Here in our limestone hills, which though pretty and private were sub-jected to agricultural ruination so long ago and so thoroughly that they're not worth trying to use intensively any more, we have so far escaped the main threat—insecticides. But in small towns not far away, where until rather recently little beat-up backyard apiaries were a common sight, only a few stubborn bee men keep trying, sorely beset by the Sevin and Malathion and chlorinated hydrocarbons with which most householders now slather their yards and gardens and trees. And in rich farming regions of the state, especially where cotton is grown and regularly dusted and sprayed, the num-ber of hives has diminished hugely since the old days. The most notable commercial honey production in Texas now, I believe, is in the brush country south and west of San Antonio, where catclaw and mesquite and guajillo and whitebrush and such things bloom in crazy profusion whenever rainfall per-mits. But even there trouble looms in the form of bulldozers clearing the land for crops or pasture grass. So maybe battered, relatively useless corners of nowhere like ours are best for keeping bees.

Uncommercially, at least. We have no blooms wild or tame that would sustain hundreds of hives in a yard or thousands through the region. In present economic terms keeping bees on a small scale doesn't really make much sense, any more than do most other small-scale rural projects. On a dozen hives, each averaging a hundred pounds' production of honey each year, which is a good bit more than I usually get but not as much as a more dedicated apiarist can expect, you can gross at present bulk wholesale prices about six hundred dollars. This can be upped considerably by peddling bottled honey around and swinging whatever retail sales you can. But when you put your hours and your investment in equipment in the balance, you'll probably find you'd have been better off sacking groceries or digging post holes for hire.

On the other hand Winnebagos and season tickets at the Astrodome don't make much economic sense either, and they require a good bit more outlay in both time and cash, from those who cherish them, than do we rustics' undomesticated, melliferous bugs. Therefore the hell with economic sense, at any rate in terms of bees. Our bones well know, if our brains do not, that dollar values have nothing to do with the pleasure of watching the hives' intricate functioning through the seasons, of botanizing pragmatically or otherwise, of storing up great jugs and carboys of precious golden stuff and using it during the year and giving it away at Christmas, of making mead, of catching swarms and the rest.

Not to mention all those free stings one gets for one's arthritis.

Blue and Some Other Dogs

One cool still night last March, when the bitterest winter in decades was starting to slack its grip and the first few chuck-will's-widows were whistling tentative claims to nest territories, the best dog I ever owned simply disappeared. Dogs do disappear, of course. But not usually dogs like Blue or under conditions like ours here in the cedar hills.

A crossbred sheep dog, he had spent his whole ten years of life on two North Texas country places and had not left the vicinity of the house at either of them without human company since the age of two or less, when his mother was still alive and we also had an aging and lame and anarchic dachshund who liked to tempt the two of them out roaming after armadillos and feral cats and raccoons and other varmints. This happened usually at night when we'd neglected to bring the dachshund into the house, or he had tricked his way outside by faking a call of nature or pushing open an unlatched screen door. The dachshund, named Watty (it started as Cacahuate or Peanut), had a very good nose and the two sheep dogs didn't, and having located quarry for them he would scream loud sycophantic applause as they pursued it and attacked, sometimes mustering the courage to run in and bite an exposed hind leg while the deadly mother and son kept the front part occupied.

It was fairly gory at times, and I'm not all that much at war with varmints except periodically with individual specimens that have developed a taste for chickens or kid goats or garden corn. In fact, I rather like having them around. But the main problem was the roaming itself, which sometimes took the dogs a mile or so from home and onto other property. In the country wandering dogs are an abomination, usually in time shifting their attention from wild prey to poultry and sheep and goats and calves, and nearly always dying sooner or later from a rifle bullet or buckshot or poison bait, well enough deserved. Few people have lived functionally on the land without having to worry sooner or later about such raiders, and the experience makes them jumpy about their own dogs' habits. Thus they find much irony in city visitors' standard observation that country dogs are very lucky to have so much space for roving and playing.

To cope, you can chain or pen your dogs when they aren't with you, or you can teach them to stay at home. While I favor the latter approach, with three dogs on hand and one of them a perverse and uncontrollable old house pet too entwined with my own past and with the family to get rid of, it was often hard to make training stick. At least it was until the dachshund perished under the wheels of a pickup truck, his presence beneath it unsuspected by the driver and his cranky senile arrogance too great to let him scuttle out of the way when the engine started.

Blue's mother was a brindle-and-white Basque sheep dog from Idaho, of a breed said to be called Pannish, though you can't prove that by me since I've never seen another specimen. Taut and compact and aggressive, she was quick to learn but also quick to spot ways to nudge rules aside or to get out of work she didn't savor. She came to us mature and a bit over-disciplined, and if you tried to teach her a task too roughly she would refuse permanently to have anything to do with it. I ruined her for cow work by whipping her for running a heifer through a net fence for the hell of it, and ever afterward if I started dealing with cattle when she was with me, she would go to heel or disappear. Once while chousing a neighbor's Herefords out of an oat patch toward the spate-ripped fence watergap through which they had invaded it, I looked around for Pan and glimpsed her peeking at me slyly from a shin oak thicket just beyond the field's fringe, hiding there till the risk of being called on for help was past.

Not that she feared cows or anything else that walked—or crawled or flew or swam or for that matter rolled on wheels. She attacked strange dogs like a male and had a contemptuous hatred of snakes that made her bore straight in to grab them and shake them dead, even after she had been bitten twice by rattlers, once badly. After such a bout I've seen her with drops of amber venom rolling down her shoulder where fangs had struck the thick fine hair but had failed to reach her skin. Occasionally she bit people too, always men, though she was nervous enough around unfamiliar children that we never trusted her alone with them. Women, for her own secret reasons, she liked more or less indiscriminately.

She was a sort of loaded weapon, Pan, and in town there would have been no sense in keeping such a dog around, except maybe to patrol fenced grounds at night. But we were living then on a leased place just beyond the western honky-tonk fringe of Fort Worth, where drunken irrationals roved the byways after midnight, and I was often away. There, what might otherwise have been her worst traits were re-assuring. She worshiped my wife and slept beside the bed when I was gone, and would I am certain have died in defense of the household with the same driven ferocity she showed in combat with wild things.

A big boar coon nearly got her one January night, before she had Blue to help her out. The old dachshund sicked her on it by the barn, where it had come for a bantam supper, and by the time I had waked to the noise and pulled on pants and located a flashlight, the fight had rolled down to the creek and Pan's chopping yap had suddenly stilled, though Watty was still squalling hard. When I got there and shone the light on a commotion in the water, all that showed was the coon's solemn face and his shoulders. Astraddle Pan's neck with an ear clutched in each hand, he was quite competently holding her down despite her mightiest struggles; big bubbles rolled up as I watched with dachshund Watty dancing yet up-roarious beside me on good firm land. Grabbing up a stick I waded into the frigid chest-deep pool, whacked the coon out of his saddle, declined his offer to climb me in retaliation, and sent him swimming somewhat groggily for the other bank. But by then Pan was unconscious, and on shore I shook and pumped the better part of a gallon of water out of her before she started to wheeze and cough. Which didn't keep her from tearing into the very next coon her brave, small, black friend sniffed out, though I don't recall her ever following another one into water. She was not too rash to learn what an im-possibility was.

We had a plague of feral housecats at that place, strayed outward from the city or dumped along the roads by the kind of people who do that sort of thing, and a huge tom one time gave the dachshund his comeuppance. After a notable scrap with Pan the tom decided to leave as I arrived, but she grabbed him by the tail as he went. At this point old Watty, thinking in dim light that the customary face-to-face encounter was still in progress and gaining from my arrival the courage the cat had lost, dashed in for a furtive chomp and was received in a loving, tight, clawed embrace with sharp teeth in its middle. His dismay was piercingly loud and he bore those scars for life. . . . The tomcat got away, wiser too I suspect.

If my less than objective interest in these violent matters is evident, I have the grace to be a bit ashamed of it, but not much. I have friends among the hound-dog men whose main pleasure in life lies in fomenting such pursuits and brawls, and some of them are very gentle people—i.e., I am not of the school that believes hunting per se makes worse brutes of men than they already are, or ever did or ever will. Though I still hunt a little myself, I don't hunt in that way, and these home-ground uproars I seldom encouraged except occasionally much later, when Blue had become our only dog and had constituted himself our Protector of Garden and Poultry. The toll of wildlife actually killed over the years was light, reaching a mild peak during the brief period after Blue was full grown and before Pan died, when they hunted and fought as a skill-ful team. Most chases would end with a treeing and I would go and call the dogs home with no blood spilled on either side. But Man the Hunter's association with dogs is very very long-standing, and anyone who can watch a slashing battle between his own dogs and something wild and tough, when it does occur, without feeling a flow of the old visceral reckless joy, is either quite skilled at suppressing his emotions or more dif-ferent from me than I think most men are.

There being of course the additional, more primary and cogent fact that in the country varmints around the house and barn and chicken yard are bad news, and the best help in keeping them away, if you dislike poison and traps and such things, is aggressive dogs. They can give you a bad turn on occasion, though, as Pan did one evening when she assailed something in a tight V-mesh fence corner and, hearing high shrill yipes, I thought she was murdering a friend and neighbor's treasured tiny poodle, a wide wanderer named Pierre. I ran out and yanked her away, and out came not Pierre but a quite rumpled little gray fox, who did not give his name but streaked off to safety.

Unable to find any males of Pan's breed in this region, we mated her with one of those more numerous sheep dogs, similar in build and coat but colored white and black-speckled gray, known as Queensland Blue Heelers or more commonly just as Australians. Three of the resultant pups had her hue and the fourth was Blue, marked like his sire but with less speckling and no trace of the blue "glass" or "china" tinge that many, perhaps most Australians have in one or both eyes, sometimes as only a queer pale blaze on an iris. When the time came to choose, we picked him to keep, and as a result he turned out to be a far different sort of grown dog than he would have if we had given him away.

For Pan was an impossibly capricious, domineering mother, neurotic in her protectiveness but punitive toward the pups to the point of drawing blood when they annoyed her, which was often. The others got out from under at six or eight weeks of age, but Blue had to stay and take it, and kept on taking it until Pan died—run over too, while nudging at the rule against chasing cars. Even after he had reached full size, at seventy-five pounds half again bigger than either Pan or his sire, he had to be always on the watch for her unforeseeable snarling fits of displeasure.

I used to wish he would round on her and whip her hard once and for all, but he never did. Instead he developed the knack of turning clownish at a moment's notice, reverting to ingratiating puppy tricks to deflect the edge of her wrath. He would run around in senseless circles yapping, would roll on his back with his feet wiggling in the air, and above all would grin—crinkle his eyes and turn up the corners of his mouth and loll his tongue out over genially bared teeth. It was a travesty of all mashed-down human beings who have had to clown to survive, like certain black barbershop shoeshine "boys," some of them sixty years old, whom I remember from my youth.

These antics worked well enough with Pan that they became a permanent part of the way Blue was, and he brought them to his relationship with people, mainly me, where they worked also. It was quite hard to stay angry at a large strong dog, no matter what he had just done, who had his bobtailed butt in the air and his head along his forelegs on the ground and his eyes skewed sidewise at you as he smiled a wide, mad, minstrel-show smile. If I did manage to stay angry despite all, he would most often panic and flee to his hideout beneath the pickup's greasy differential, which may have been another effect of Pan's gentle motherliness or may just have been Australian; they are sensitive dogs, easily cowed, and require light handling. For the most part, all that Blue did require was light handling, for he wanted immensely to please and was the easiest dog to train in standard matters of behavior that I have ever had to deal with. Hating cats, for instance, he listened to one short lecture concerning a kitten just purchased by my small daughters for twenty-five cents at a church benefit sale, and not only let her alone thereafter but became her staunchest friend, except perhaps in the matter of tomcats she might have favored, which he kept on chasing off. And he learned things like heeling in two hours of casual coaching.

Which harks back to my description of him as the best dog

I ever owned. He was. But it is needful at this point to confess that that is not really saying much. Nearly all the dogs I owned before Blue and Pan and Watty were pets I had as a boy in Fort Worth, a succession of fox terriers and curs and whatnot that I babied, teased, cajoled, overfed, and generally spoiled in the anthropomorphic manner of kids everywhere. Most perished young, crushed by cars, and were mourned with tears and replaced quite soon by others very much like them in undisciplined worthlessness. In those years I consumed with enthusiasm Jack London's dog books and other less sinewy stuff like the works of Albert Payson Terhune, with their tales of noble and useful canines, but somehow I was never vouchsafed the ownership of anything that faintly resembled Lad or Buck or White Fang.

The best of the lot was a brown-and-white mongrel stray that showed up already old and gray-chopped, with beautiful manners and training, but he liked grownups better than children and stayed with my father when he could. The worst but most beloved was an oversized Scotty named Roderick Dhu, or Roddy, who when I was twelve or thirteen or so used to accompany me and a friend on cumbersome hunting and camping expeditions to the Trinity West Fork bottom beyond the edge of town, our wilderness. He had huge negative will power and when tired or hot would often sit down and refuse to move another inch. Hence from more than one of those forays I came hiking back out of the valley burdened not only with a Confederate bedroll, a canteen, a twenty-two rifle, a bowie knife, an ax, a frying pan, and other such impedimenta, but with thirty-five deadweight pounds of warm dog as well.

The friend's dog in contrast was a quick bright feist called Buckshot, destined to survive not only our childhood but our college years and the period when we were away at the war and nearly a decade longer, dying ultimately, my friend swears, at the age of twenty-two. A canine wraith, nearly blind and grayed all over and shrunken, he would lie in corners and dream twitching of old possums and rabbits we had harried through the ferns and poison ivy, thumping his tail on the floor when human movement was near if he chanced to be awake.

With this background, even though I knew about useful dogs from having had uncles and friends who kept them for hunting and from having seen good herd dogs at work during country work in adolescence, as well as from reading, I arrived at my adult years with a fairly intact urban, middleclass, sentimental ideal of the Nice Dog, a cleancut fellow who obeyed a few selected commands, was loyal and gentle with his masters, and refrained conscientiously from "bad" behavior as delineated by the same said masters. I had never had one and knew it, and the first dog I owned after years of unsettled existence was the dachshund Watty, who was emphatically not one either.

He started out all right, intelligent and affectionate and as willing to learn as dachshunds ever are, and with the nose he had he made a fair retriever, albeit hardmouthed with shot birds and inclined to mangle them a bit before reluctantly giving them up. He was fine company too, afield or in a boat or a car, and we had some good times together, even collaborating on a book about a float trip we made down the Brazos River. But his temper started souring when I married, and grew vile when children came, and the job was finished by a paralyzing back injury with a long painful recovery, never complete, and by much sympathetic spoiling along the way. As an old lame creature, a stage that lasted at least five years, he snarled, bit, disobeyed, stank more or less constantly and from time to time broke wind to compound it, yowled and barked for his supper in the kitchen for two hours before feeding time, subverted the good sheep dogs' training, and was in general the horrid though small-scale antithesis of a Nice Dog. And yet in replication of my childhood self I loved him, and buried him wrapped in a feed sack beneath a flat piece of limestone with his name scratched deep upon it.

(While for Blue, than whom I will never have a Nicer Dog even if perhaps one more useful, there is no marker at all because there is no grave on which to put one . . .)

I do think Watty knocked out of me most of my residual kid sentimentality about dogs in general—he along with living in the country where realism is forced on you by things like having to cope with goat-killing packs of sterling canines, and the experience of having the sheep dogs with their strong thrust and potential, never fully attained—to the point that I'm certain I will never put up with an unmanageable dog again. I remember one time of sharp realization during the second summer after we had bought this cedar-hill place, long before we lived here any part of the year or even used it for grazing. That spring after the dachshund had been thrown from the pickup's seat when I jammed on the brakes in traffic, I had carried him partly paralyzed to the vet, a friend, who advised me frankly that the smart thing would be a lethal painless shot of pentothal. But he added that he had always wanted to try to cure one of those tricky dachshund spines, and that if I would go along with him he'd charge me only his actual costs. Though by that time Watty was already grumpy and snappish and very little pleasure to have around, sentimentality of course triumphed over smart. The trouble was that with intensive therapy still going strong after several weeks, "actual costs" were mounting absurdly, to the point that even now in far costlier times I can grunt when I think of them.

Engaged that summer in some of the endless construction that has marked our ownership of the place, I was in and out every day or so with loads of lumber and cement and things, and paused sometimes to talk with a pleasant man who lived on the road I used. He had a heterogeneous troop of dogs around the yard, some useful and some just there, their ringleader a small white cur with pricked ears and redrimmed eyes who ran cars and was very noisy, but was prized by the man's children and had the redeeming trait of being, quote, hell at finding rattlesnakes.

One morning as I drove in, this dog was sitting upright under a liveoak fifty yards short of the house, with his head oddly high and askew. He had found one snake too many. His eyes were nearly shut and on the side of his neck was a lump about the size of his head. Nor did he acknowledge my passage with as much as a stifled yip. Thinking perhaps they didn't know, I stopped by the house.

"Yes," said my friend. "He run onto a big one up by the tank yesterday evening and by the time I got there with a hoe it had done popped him good."

"Did you do anything for him?"

"Well, we put some coal oil on it," he said. "I was going to cut it open but there's all those veins and things. You know they say if a snake hits a dog in the body he's a goner, but if it's the head he'll get all right. You reckon the neck's the head?"

I said I hoped so, and for days as I passed in and out I watched the little dog under his oak, from which he did not stir, and checked with the family about him. They were not at all indifferent; he was a main focus of interest and they kept fresh food and water by him. The neck swelled up still fatter and broke open, purging terrible fluids. After this happened he seemed to feel better and even ate a little, but then one morning he was dead. Everyone including me was sad that he had lost his fight to live, and the children held a funeral for him, with bouquets of wild prairie pinks.

And such was my changing view that it seemed somehow

to make more healthy sense than all that cash I was ramming into a spoiled irascible dachshund's problematic cure. . . .

"Good" country dogs are something else, and are often treated like members of the family and worried over as much when sick. This is not sentimentality but hard realism, because they're worth worrying over in pragmatic terms. There aren't very many of them. As good dogs always have, they come mainly from ruthless culling of promising litters and from close careful training, and most belong to genuine stockmen with lots of herding work to do. These owners routinely turn down offers of a thousand or more dollars for them, if you believe the stories, as you well may after watching a pair of scroungy border collies, in response to a low whistle or a word, run a half-mile up a brush-thick pasture and bring back seventy-nine Angora wethers and pack them into a fence corner or a pen for shearing, doctoring, or loading into a trailer, all while their master whittles a mesquite twig to a point and picks his teeth with it.

Blue wasn't that kind of dog or anywhere near it, nor was there much chance to develop such talent on a place like ours, where the resident cows and goats are fairly placid and few problems in handling them emerge that can't be solved with a little patience and a rattling bucket of feed. For that matter, I don't know nearly enough about the training of such dogs to have helped him get to be one, though a livestock buyer I know, who has superb dogs himself and handles thousands of sheep and goats each year on their way from one owner to another, did tell me after watching Blue try to help us one morning that if I'd let him have him for six months, he might be able to "make a dog out of him." I was grateful and thought it over but in the end declined, partly because I mistrusted what six months of training by a stranger might do to that queer, one-man, nervous Australian streak in Blue, but mainly because I didn't know what I'd do with such a dog if I had him, in these rather miniature and unstrenuous livestock operations. His skills would rust unused, and the fact I had to face was that I didn't deserve a dog like that.

What Blue amounted to, I guess, was a country Nice Dog, which in terms of utility is a notable cut above the same thing in the city. These dogs stay strictly at home without being tied or penned, announce visitors, keep varmints and marauding dogs and unidentified nocturnal boogers away, cope with snakes (Blue, after one bad fanging that nearly killed him, abandoned his dam's tactics of headlong assault and would circle a snake raising hell till I came to kill it, or to call him off if it was harmless), watch over one's younger children, and are middling to good help at shoving stock through a loading chute or from one pen to another, though less help in pastures where the aiming point may be a single gate in a long stretch of fence and judgment is required. Some learn simple daily herding tasks like bringing in milk cows at evening, though I've observed that much of the time these tasks involve an illusion on the part of the dog and perhaps his owner that he is making cows or goats or sheep do something, when actually they have full intention of doing it on their own, unforced. Or the whole thing may be for fun, as it was with one old cowman I knew, who had an ancient collie named Babe. When visitors came to sit with the old man on his porch, he would at some point level a puzzled blue glare across the pasture and say in conversational tones, "I declare, Babe, it looks like that old mare has busted out of the corral again. Maybe you better bring her in." And Babe would rise and go do as he had been bidden and the visitors would be much impressed, unless they happened to be aware that it was the one sole thing he could do and that the mare was in on it too.

On the whole, to be honest, Blue was pretty poor at herding even by such lax standards—too eager and exuberant and only occasionally certain of what it was we were trying to do. But he was controllable by single words and gestures and like his mother unafraid, and in his later years when I knew his every tendency, such as nipping goats, I could correct mistakes before he made them, so that he was often of some help. He was even more often comic relief, as when a chuted cow turned fighty and loaded him into the trailer instead of he her, or when a young bull, too closely pressed, kicked him into a thick clump of scrub elm, where he landed upside down and lay stuck with his legs still running in the air. When I went over and saw that he wasn't hurt and started laughing at the way he looked, he started laughing too, at least in his own way.

For a sense of humor and of joy was the other side of that puppyish clowning streak which he always retained but which turned less defensive with time. The nervousness that went with it never left him either, but grew separate from the clowning, ritualizing itself most often in a weird habit he had of grinning and slobbering and clicking his teeth together when frustrated or perplexed. He regularly did this, for instance, when friends showed up for visits and brought their own dogs along. Knowing he wasn't supposed to attack these dogs as he did strays, Blue was uncertain what else to do with them. So he would circle them stiff-legged, wagging his stub and usually trying to mount them, male or female, small or large, and after being indignantly rebuffed would walk about popping his jaws and dribbling copious saliva. I expect some of those visiting friends thought him a very strange dog, and maybe in truth he was.

He was a bouncing, bristling, loudmouthed watchdog, bulkily impressive enough that arriving strangers would most often stay in their cars until I came out to call him off. Unlike

Pan, he bore them no real hostility and never bit anyone, though I believe that if any person or thing had threatened one of us those big white teeth would have been put to good use. Mainly, unfamiliar people disconcerted him and he wanted nothing to do with them unless I was around and showed myself receptive, at which point he was wont to start nuzzling their legs and hands like a great overgrown pup, demanding caresses. Once when the pickup was ailing I left it at a garage in town and mooched a ride home with a friend whose car Blue did not know. No one in the family was there, and when we drove up to the house there was no sign of Blue, but then I saw him peering furtively around a corner of the porch, much as his mother had eyed me from those shin oak bushes long before.

With his size, clean markings, silky thick coat, broad head, alert eyes, and usual mien of grave dignity, he was quite a noble-looking fellow. Having him along was often a social asset with strangers, even if it could turn out to be the opposite if something disturbed him and he went into his jaw-popping, drooling phase. One day when he was young and we were still living outside Fort Worth, I was apprehended in that city for running a red light, though I had thought I'd seen no light on at all when I drove through the intersection. I explained this to the arresting officer, a decent type, and together we went back and watched the damned thing run through six or eight perfectly sequenced changes from red to yellow to green and back again. Blue watched with us and, attuned to the situation, accepted a pat from the cop with an austere but friendly smile. Against pregnant silence I said with embarrassment that I guessed my eyes were failing faster than I'd thought, accepted the appropriate summons, and went my disgruntled way.

When I got home that afternoon my wife said the officer had telephoned. More decent even than I'd known, he had watched the light for a while longer by himself and had finally caught it malfunctioning, and he told Jane I could get the ticket canceled.

She thought me off in the cedar hills and believed there was some mistake. "Did he have a sheep dog in the back of the pickup?" she asked.

"No, ma'am," said Blue's till-then secret admirer. "That great big beautiful animal was sitting right up on the front seat with him."

We spent a tremendous lot of time together over the years, Blue and I— around the house and barn and pens, wandering on the place, batting about in a pickup (his pickup more than mine, for he spent much of each day inside it or beneath, even when it was parked by the house), or at farm work in the fields. When young he would follow the tractor around and around as I plowed or harrowed or sowed, but later he learned to sit under a tree and watch the work's progress in comfort, certain I was not escaping from him, though sometimes when he got bored he would bounce out to meet the tractor as it neared him and would try to lead it home. Fond of the whole family and loved by all, he would go along with the girls to swim at the creek or when they went horseback across the hills, good protection for them and good company. But he needed a single main focus and I was it, so completely that at times I felt myself under surveillance. No imperfectly latched door missed his notice if I was indoors and he was out, and he could open one either by shoving or by pulling it with his teeth, as permanent marks on some of them still testify. Failing to get in, he would ascertain as best he could, by peering in windows or otherwise, just where I was located inside and then would lie down by the exterior wall closest to that spot, even if it put him in the full blast of a January norther.

At one friend's house in town that he and I used to visit

often, he would if left outside go through the attached garage to a kitchen door at odds with its jamb and seldom completely shut. Easing through it, he would traverse the breakfast room and a hall, putting one foot before another in tense slow motion, would slink behind a sofa into the living room, and using concealment as craftily as any old infantryman, would sometimes be lying beside my chair before I even knew he was in. More usually we would watch his creeping progress while pretending not to notice, and after he got where he was headed I would give him a loud mock scolding and he would roll on his back and clown, knowing he was home free and wouldn't be booted back out, as sometimes happened when he was shedding fat ticks or stinking from a recent battle with some polecat.

But there were places he wouldn't go with me, most notable among them the bee yard, his first apicultural experience having been his definite last. It happened one early spring day when I was helping a friend check through a neglected hive someone had given him and Blue had tagged along with us. The hive body and supers were badly gummed up with the tree-sap propolis bees use for glue and chinking, the combs in the frames were crooked and connected by bridge wax and tore when we took them out, and on that cool day all thirty or forty thousand workers were at home and ready to fight. They got under our veils and into all cracks in our attire, and those that didn't achieve entry just rammed their stings home through two or three layers of cloth. They also found Blue, a prime target for apian rage since they hate all hairy things, probably out of ancestral memory of hive-raiding bears. With maybe a hundred of them hung whining in his coat and stinging when they found skin, he tried to squeeze between my legs for protection and caused me to drop a frame covered with bees, which augmented the assault. Shortly thereafter, torn between mirth and pain, we gave up and slapped the hive back together and lit out at a hard run, with Blue thirty yards in front and clouds of bees flying escort. And after that whenever he saw me donning the veil and firing up my smoker, he would head in the other direction.

He did work out a method of revenge, though, which he used for the rest of his life despite scoldings and other discouragements. Finding a place where small numbers of bees were coming for some reason—a spot on the lawn where something sweet had been spilled, perhaps, or a lime-crusted dripping faucet whose flavor in their queer way they liked—he would stalk it with his special tiptoeing slink and then loudly snap bees from the air one by one as they flew, apparently not much minding the occasional stings he got on his lips and tongue. I suppose my scoldings were less severe than they ought to have been; it was a comical thing to watch and for that matter he got few bees in relation to their huge numbers, unlike another beekeeper friend's Dalmatian, afflicted with similar feelings, who used to sit all day directly in front of a hive chomping everything that flew out, and had to be given away.

Maybe Blue considered bees varmints. He took his guardianship of the home premises dead seriously and missed few creatures that came around; along with clowning, I guess this was the thing he did best. Except for the unfortunate armadillos, which he had learned to crunch, the mortality inflicted was low after Pan's death, as I've said, for most could escape through the net yard fence that momentarily blocked Blue's pursuit and few of them cared to stay and dispute matters except an occasional big squalling coon. With these we did have some rousing fine midnight fights, though I'd better not further sully my humanitarian aura, if any remains, by going into details. During the time when cantaloupes and roasting ears were coming ripe and most attractive to coons, I would leave the garden gate open at dark and Blue would go down during the night on patrol. There was sometimes a question as to whether a goodly squad of coons given full license could have done half as much damage to garden crops as the ensuing battles did, but there was no question at all about whether the procedure worked. After only two or three brawls each year, word would spread around canny coondom that large hairy danger lurked in the Graves corn patch and they would come no more, much to Blue's disappointment.

I talked to him quite a bit, for the most part childishly or joshingly as one does talk to beasts, and while I'm not idiot enough to think he "understood" any of it beyond a few key words and phrases, he knew my voice's inflections and tones, and by listening took meaning from them if meaning was there to be had, responding with a grin, a sober stare, melting affection, or some communicative panting, according to what seemed to be right. Like most dogs that converse with humans he was a thorough yes type, honoring my every point with agreement. Nice Dogs are ego boosters, and have been so since the dim red dawn of things.

I could leave him alone and untethered at the place for three or more days at a time, with dry food in a bucket under shelter and water to be had at the cattle troughs. Neighbors half a mile away have told me that sometimes when the wind was right they could hear him crooning softly wolflike, lonely, but he never left. When I came back he would be at the yard gate waiting, and as I walked toward the house he would go beside me leaping five and six feet straight up in the air in pure and utter celebration, whining and grunting maybe but seldom more; he saved loud barks for strangers and snakes and threatening varmints and such.

Last winter I slept inside the house instead of on the screen porch we shared as night quarters during much of each year unless, as often, he wanted to be outside on guard, and I hadn't moved back out by that March night when he disappeared. He had been sleeping on a horseblanket on a small open side porch facing south, and I'd begun to notice that sometimes he would be still abed and pleasantly groggy when I came out at daybreak. He was fattening a bit also, and those eyes were dimmer that once had been able to pick me out of a jostling sidewalk crowd in town and track me as I came toward the car. Because, like mine, his years were piling up. It was a sort of further bond between us.

He ate a full supper that evening and barked with authority at some coyotes singing across the creek, and in the morning was gone. I had to drive two counties north that day to pick up some grapevines and had planned to take him along. When he didn't answer my calling I decided he must have a squirrel in the elms and cedars across the house branch, where he would often sit silent and taut for hours staring up at a chattering treed rodent, oblivious to summonings and to everything else. It was a small sin that I permitted him at his age; if I wanted him I could go and search him out and bring him in, for he was never far. But that morning it didn't seem to matter and I took off without him, certain he'd be at the yard gate when I drove in after lunch, as he had invariably been over the years that had mounted so swiftly for both of us.

Except that he wasn't. Nor did a tour of his usual squirrel grounds yield any trace, or careful trudges up and down the branch, or a widening week-long search by myself and my wife and kids (whose spring vacation it used up and thoroughly ruined) that involved every brush pile and crevice we could find within half a mile or more of home, where he might have followed some coon or ringtail and then gotten stuck or been bitten in a vein by a rattler just out of its long winter's doze and full of rage and venom. Or watching for the tight downspiral of feeding buzzards. Or driving every road in the county twice or more and talking with people who, no, had not seen any dogs like that or even any bitches in heat that might have passed through recruiting. Or ads run in the paper and notices taped to the doors of groceries and feed mills, though these did produce some false hopes that led me up to thirty miles away in vain.

Even his friend the two-bit cat, at intervals for weeks, would sit and meow toward the woods in queer and futile lament. . . .

I ended fairly certain of what I'd surmised from the start, that Blue lay dead, from whatever cause, beneath some thick heap of bulldozed brush or in one of those deep holes, sometimes almost caves, that groundwater eats out under the limestone ledges of our hills. For in country as brushy and wrinkled and secret as this we can't have found all of such places roundabout, even fairly close.

Or maybe I want to believe this because it has finality.

And maybe he will still turn up, like those long-lost animals you read about in children's books and sometimes in newspaper stories.

He won't.

And dogs are nothing but dogs and I know it better than most, and all this was for a queer and nervous old crossbreed that couldn't even herd stock right. Nor was there anything humanly unique about the loss, or about the emptiness that came in the searching's wake, which comes sooner or later to all people foolish enough to give an animal space in their lives. But if you are built to be such a fool, you are, and if the animal is to you what Blue was to me the space he leaves empty is big.

It is partly filled for us now by a successor, an Old English pup with much promise—sharp and alert, wildly vigorous but responsive and honest, puppy-absurd but with an underlying gravity that will in time I think prevail. There is nothing nervous about him; he has a sensitivity that could warp in that direction if mishandled, but won't if I can help it. Nor does he show any fear beyond healthy puppy caution, and in the way he looks at cows and goats and listens to people's words I see clearly that he may make a hell of a dog, quite possibly better than Blue. Which is not, as I said, saying much . . .

But he isn't Blue. In the domed shape of his head under my hand as I sit reading in the evenings I can still feel that broader, silkier head, and through his half-boisterous, half-bashful, glad morning hello I still glimpse Blue's clown grin and crazy leaps. I expect such intimate remembrance will last a good long while, for I waited the better part of a lifetime to own a decent dog, and finally had him, and now don't have him any more. And I resolve that when this new one is grown and more or less shaped in his ways, I am going to get another pup to raise beside him, and later maybe a third. Because I don't believe I want to face so big a dose of that sort of emptiness again.

Some Chickens
I Have Known

As an abject devotee of country how-to-do-it books, I possess
several volumes with titles like *The Home Chicken Flock*,
Starting Right with Poultry, and *Chickens for Fun and Profit*.
As their names indicate, these are earnest homely treatises
aimed at backyarders and small-farm owners, and I have read
them all with the careful interest that we self-sufficiency enthusiasts, however impure, reserve for such material. I therefore know a certain amount about hen yards and laying houses
and droppings pits and the spacing of roost poles, and over
a period of time have acquired or constructed a few bits of
relevant hardware like waterers, feeders, brood coops, and so
on. But somehow, despite good intentions formed while read-

ing beside a winter fire, the use I've made of this information and equipment has been incomplete and fitful and not in general zealous.

The notion has sometimes whispered itself to me that maybe I'm just not a Chicken Fun and Profit type. . . . Yet we have always had some chickens around, half-wild for the most part, and quite aside from enjoying what good rich red-yolked eggs we can find and an occasional free-ranging fryer, we have come to count on them as an integral part of our surroundings. I seldom consciously notice the crowing of roosters at dawn, for instance, but when I wake up elsewhere I consciously notice its absence, and miss it. And over the years the view from my office window here at the rear of the barn would have been a poorer one without periodic glimpses of alfresco cockfights, or of some old game biddy with her chicks as she chases and spears and dismembers small quarry of various sorts, sharing out bugs and tarantula legs and lizard entrails and clucking with crazy glee to indicate how very nutritious they are.

What I know I'm not is a scientific poultry-management aficionado. I had a couple of books on that subject too, bought by error and given away soon after I'd explored their contents. Polemicists have declaimed in print against the inhumanity of confining birds by the scores of thousands to mesh-floored cages from the moment of their miraculous emergence from the egg to that dark time when they are efficiently killed and plucked and gutted and shunted to market as corpses pallid with fat, certified disease-free because of the antibiotics they have gobbled up with their mash. And have inveighed against keeping laying hens in much the same fashion, bumfoozling them into extra egg production with eternal electric light. I have nothing to add on this subject, maybe in part because one of the nicest things about chickens is that it's rather hard to get emotionally involved with them, and inhumanity toward the idiotic breeds of fowl that have practically been manufactured for such industrial use, if it is inhumanity, hardly seems worth getting worked up about. Not that I wouldn't rather eat the other kind of chickens and the other kind of eggs, but that's for empirical reasons, because they're healthier and taste a whole lot better.

My objections to participation in such poultry-management practices are also empirical, based on two or three swatches of clear-eyed observation. One such occurred not long after World War II, when with a friend from college days I took a tour around Texas to look up old companions and to find out how they had weathered the hectic years since graduation. By and large, we found that those we could locate had weathered them much as we had—i.e., with emotional development arrested as of circa 1942 and with a degree of confusion as to what all the intervening military brouhaha had meant to them, if anything, but with an exceeding willingness to drink beer and strong waters and to swap war stories. The zigzag trip lasted for weeks and stretched from the High Plains to the Gulf Coast by way of various ranches, honky-tonks, large and dignified homes, Guadalupe riverbottom fishing shacks, motel rooms, and other stopping points. And at one stage we conferred the blessing of our presence on two old classmates, married by then and less confused than most of us or so at first it seemed, who had allied themselves against the future by acquiring and modernizing a broiler operation on two or three acres of land not far from the shining towers of Waco.

For that time, I suppose it was a fair-sized endeavor, with a flow-through population of perhaps nine or ten thousand birds funneling in one end as downy chicks and out the other as meat. Big and sophisticated in comparison to the "chicken farms" that during the Depression and on briefly into postwar years constituted a retirement dream for multitudes of thirty-year military types and other pensioners, it was a diminutive forerunner of the enormous corporate operations which today have driven most individual owners out of the poultry game. It occupied some long tin sheds whose grayed roofs shimmered under the Texas sun and from whose raised flap windows flowed the massed gabble of those thousands of perverted and nervous birds, as well as the massed pungency of their droppings. The weather was hot, without much wind, and if an instrument for measuring the intensity of odor exists, as it well may for all I know, and had been focused on that operation or on any point within the small, stucco, unairconditioned house that had come with the property and was now sheltering both our friends plus wives plus one small baby, it would most certainly have exploded. Nor, in my scant experience, is it possible to ignore or get used to the scent of chicken manure—as one can ignore and sometimes like, for instance, equivalent emanations from horses and cows or even, according to the biased testimony of some pig-fancying friends of mine, from swine.

They had all their capital in the thing, about ten thousand dollars each, which one had inherited and the other had earned playing murderous poker as a naval officer on a troopship. Newcastle disease or something like that had obliterated three or four months' hypothetical profit just prior to our arrival. Dislike circulated back and forth between the wives, one a loud-voiced forthright good old girl and the other a ladylike blonde with an Eastern college degree. Automation being not yet even a word, much hard hot day-and-night work was required, and everybody was eating chicken twice a day in the absence of funds for more varied provender. But that was just as well because anything else they might have cooked up would have tasted like chicken poot too, since that was all you could smell.

Some Chickens I Have Known

We stayed two nights on a hideaway sofa-bed, listening in the small hours through thin walls to a sweaty baby's howling and to the blonde girl's occasional pillow-dulled sobs, and a week later and a hundred and fifty miles away my suitcase still had the stink of that place inside it. Our friends lasted there not a great while longer. One of the marriages crumpled under the strain—oddly, I believe it was the good old girl who left—and the operation was sold off at a large loss, and the two former college roomies went their separate ways toward less idyllic pursuits.

Whether it's experiences like that one that have spoiled me for careful chicken husbandry even on a homestead scale, or some atavistic backwash in my psyche, the fact is that so far the only sort of chickens I've had any luck with or cared much about are those that more or less take care of themselves. This attitude was reinforced by an effort I once made to keep a few purebred bantams in an orderly and protected way, maybe out of memories of childhood when my father maintained a gentle, pampered bunch of Golden Sebrights on our back lot. But the bantams' eggs were tiny and the cockerels when I bothered to fix them for the table were not much bigger than very lean quail, though coons and ringtails and other wild carnivores found them delicious and very easy to catch. Not having yet learned to accept such raiding in stride, I took each loss to heart. I remember going out once at dawn to see about a commotion in the little plywood hovel I'd built for them, and finding that during the night a skunk had broken in and killed my rooster and some hens, eating only their heads as is the mustelines' frequent and peculiar custom. The scene held a sort of Oriental tragic magnificence, with the monarch and three of his wives lying gorily decapitated on the throne-room floor while the rest of the harem ran around in circles and screamed about their loss, or maybe just about their fear. But mainly what its magnificence roused in me was the rage of a bilked peasant; I was not far in spirit from those Chaucerian villagers who with clubs and trumpets ran and "skriked and howped" vainly behind Russell the fox as he dashed off with cock Chantecleer in his jaws, except that there was nothing to skrike at. Despite a heavy teaching schedule at the time, I sat up a good part of the next night at the open kitchen window with a shotgun, and in cold moonlight blasted the foul regicide when he came back for more heads. This gave me some good solid peasant satisfaction, but before long it was there to do over again, and in the end I gave what bantams were left to a friend's grandson, along with their rickety house.

Even so, I do still have an intermittent vision (by that same fire in winter) of an ample run and a neat hen house, heavily fenced and electrified against predatory intruders and stocked with fat motherly Buff Orpingtons who will stroll and scratch sedately and chortle with happiness and lay large numbers of huge brown eggs. But for now, all I've got is fighting games that hide their few eggs in very funny places, soil our porches, chase cats, roost in the barn's rafters to the detriment of things below, run like chaparral cocks, and fly like pheasants.

We came by our original batch of games through accident—inheritance, I guess you could call it. When first married we lived in a renovated white Prairie Gothic farmhouse west of Fort Worth, with a barn nearby that was leased out separately as a boarding stable. The stable declined from grace as it passed out of the hands of the local horsey set, folks with pretty longlegged steeds and jodhpurs and Italian forward-seat jumping saddles and social heft, and became gradually but inexorably a haunt of goat ropers with their tight-pants girls and their hangers-on. One major sign of change was the appearance of a little flock of game hens with one big clipped-comb rooster, released there for toughening by the chicken-fighting goat roper who owned them. When that phase of the stable's existence ended, as end it did when the debt-ridden lessee bailed out for California with a lady not his wife, this sport came one night with his chromed pickup and some friends and flashlights and recaptured his birds from limbs and rafters where they were roosting, and took them away.

But he missed one large red hen who had made a nest in the loft from which she later hatched ten chicks. She was a tremendous mother and could ride a hungry cat or a nosy dog for fifty yards, spurring and pecking it all the way; our dachshund reached the point that he'd refuse to go out if she was around the yard, preferring constipation to her ire. But the odds were rough against her in that deserted barn. By the time the Norway rats and the night creatures got through she had one offspring left, a skittish black rooster who when nearly grown managed one day to fly his head into a dangling noose of baling wire at the entrance to a stall and hanged himself as neatly as any executioner could have. So that Big Mama, as we called her admiringly from afar, was yet again alone.

When we moved not long afterward to a larger holding farther out from town, I went down and grabbed Big Mama off her roost, getting spurred on the thumb in the process, and carried her out to the new place where there were four or five mixed-blood hens, part game themselves, and a chunky Dominicker-looking rooster. Big Mama promptly whipped them all including the cock, but she was willing enough to use him for her main purpose of propagation, and during her prime at that place she hatched one or two broods each year, losing a majority of the chicks except when occasionally, goaded by conscientiousness, I caught her and forced her to hatch and partly raise them in a coop.

The other hens also reproduced themselves, though with less dedication and success. Sometimes, despite the constant depredations of foxes and coons and skunks and owls and ringtails and possums and rats and snakes and feral cats (themselves all constantly subject to attack by our dogs; it was a good steady interesting uproar), we had as many as twenty hens, lots of daily eggs searched out by the children, and a spotty supply of fat cockerels for the skillet. The Home Chicken Flock, unmanaged . . . With such stark Darwinism at work, Big Mama's bellicose genes soon came to predominate, though somewhere along the way she herself vanished in the night. We did get infusions of fresh blood from time to time, mainly through gift chickens that had outgrown their attractiveness as pets in town. One such was Whitey Corder, an erstwhile purple Easter chick metamorphosed into a large ill-natured Leghorn; his main trouble was that like many pets reared out of touch with their own kind he thought he was a person. That was all right until he started trying to mount small visiting girls and ended up in a pot with dumplings, which is about the only way you can eat a full-grown rooster and enjoy it, if you can at all.

This tough and fluctuating and motley flock persisted until the last couple of years of our tenancy at that place, when we and our dogs began spending the summers down here on our own cedar-hill acreage fifty miles away, and the chickens were left for three months at a time without even the casual protection of our presence. The last survivor was a lean black hen, a fit daughter to Big Mama, who kept on laying and hopefully incubating unfertilized eggs even after something chewed a big hunk out of her breast one night. She succumbed in the end to a five-millimeter pellet fired by an irate gardener living half a mile away, to whom I had given permission for such action after she ate all his cherry tomatoes.

Here on our own ground where we finally moved a few years ago, my intention at the start was to run a fairly taut ship and not to undertake any given homestead activity until I was ready to do it right. Sometimes things have worked out that way, but I fear that more often they haven't. Available time and flagging personal vigor are prickly factors, and long observation of one's fellow rustics and their time-honored ways also nudges one toward a slobbish conviction that rightness and taut ships are after all relative things. It's better, for instance, to have a garden full of johnsongrass roots and resprouting brush that have to be fought back among the vegetables each year, than to have no garden at all. And even though one may nurse within one's secret winter-fireside self a vision of fat Orpingtons adeptly tended, does that mean perforce that one must do without fresh eggs and morning cock-crows till the requisite facilities have been built?

When tempted early on—in fact, before we even moved here to stay—I decided that it didn't. While visiting a South Texas friend I ventured to admire a resident flock of what he called scrub Mexican games, as tough and self-reliant a crew as old Big Mama's get but uniform in type, the cocks of the coloration known as black-breasted red which traces straight back to the Asian junglefowl ancestral to all chickens, and the hens neatly brown with golden-tan speckles and shadings. He asked if I'd like a trio—two hens and a rooster, the standard small-scale "start" with poultry. Subverting yet once more the Orpington Dream, I said swiftly that I would, and from that action derives, these ten years later or so, our present teeming flock of chickens, numbering two.

Not that they haven't thrived at times, to the point that I gave away a good many to other people myself, thus in effect repaying the original gift. One trio went to a local young townsman, whose subsequent experience indicated that my friend's description of their lineage might be slightly awry. They may or may not be Mexican, but there is nothing scrub about them. This boy said he just wanted to raise a flock for fun and I believe he really did, but a chicken-fighting crony (our region has more than its share of these) persuaded him to trim the cock's comb and wattles and fit him with steel spurs, and the first Sunday that they fought him he murdered his adversary in short order and won them sixty dollars. Unfortunately this was his last fight, for shortly thereafter a red fox invaded the pasture cowshed where they were keeping him with the hens, and bore him away to the brush for dinner, all while the distraught owner was running toward the shed and waving a stick and skriking and howping. Thus perish human hopes and dreams.

Around here we've had some fairly impressive cockfights too, mainly in years when I've neglected to harvest the new generation of cockerels soon enough; it takes a twenty-two and a certain amount of stalking and I sometimes put it off. When the sexual itch begins to gnaw them they get to squabbling among themselves for rank, and some reach the point of wanting to try Papa on for size, nearly always a mistake. Once committed to battle, they only rarely quit unless blinded or totally outclassed in weight and age, and if you break up the brawl they will resume it later elsewhere. Winners lack entirely that forbearance that characterizes bulls and billy-goats and most other animal victors in struggles for dominance, who let the loser shamble away in battered disgruntlement. A gamecock will keep on pecking and spurring a downed opponent while there's a twitch still visible, and when the twitches stop he climbs on top of the bloody corpse and

crows, staggering with fatigue and with the weakness of his own wounds.

They are in short not very nice fellows, but then they're not supposed to be. What you tend to forget if you keep them just as chickens, watching them chase grasshoppers about the yard and strut for the hens and arch their necks to crow picturesquely from time to time, is that for hundreds and maybe thousands of years game fowl have been bred by men for a single main fell purpose, so that their ferocity far exceeds that of their wild progenitors and is in a sense not so much their own as an extension of human ferocity, which may well be the worst kind of all.

But when I'm honest with myself I know their ferocity is damned beautiful as well, because in another sense what men have bred into them over the centuries is an ideal of total courage. . . .

Total courage in relation to other chickens, however, is not much of a defense against toothed nocturnal varmints, and in the past couple of years some individual canny marauder, probably a fox but maybe a coon, has whittled our flock down from a peak population of around two dozen to one rooster and one hen. He has accomplished this on regular tours of their chosen center, the barn, by finding and carrying off every hen whose instincts have brought her down out of the rafters to set a clutch of eggs in some low nook or corner, except for this last one, who somehow escaped when he destroyed her nest last spring and has not since let instinct betray her again, though sooner or later I guess it will. Of dogs we have at present one large, fat, and exceptionally benevolent pup who so far thinks that all creatures wild and tame were created as playmates for him. But even when old Blue the varmint-hater was still around, the barn was too far from the house to be included in his night-time patrolling orbit.

So the games are on their own as they pretty much always

have been, but this time the arithmetic is very poor. Before long, I suspect, I'll find it needful to set aside my admiration for them as natural creatures and my disinclination to interfere in natural processes, at least as far as chickens are concerned, and will engage in a little management with some traps and a shotgun and flashlight. Otherwise it might turn out to be time to build that neat hen house with its yard and to get those Orpingtons—and, strangely, I don't really seem to want to. This has little to do with the work that would be involved, for construction around here is more or less constant anyhow. What I find with surprise, when I dig down to the bottom of my feelings on the subject, is a very strong doubt that those fat and motherly creatures would be half as much pleasure to own and to watch as the wild and raunchy birds we have grown used to over the years.

Starting Right with Poultry is undoubtedly a great idea. But starting wrong and keeping on that way may suit some of us better.

Ponderings, People,
and Other Oddments

Noticing

A good long while back as time goes for us individual mortals, I lived for slightly more than a year in a small dingy apartment on East Fifteenth Street in New York City, poking more or less continually at the keys of a Corona portable and hoping for better days ahead. While Manhattan has never been exactly my idea of a spiritual home, I think I was farther from considering it one that year than during any of several other stays, even if it did give me what I was looking for when I went there: anonymity, release from the pressures of family and friends, mental scope for some knotty apprentice work.

My sixth-floor windows in that habitation gave onto an

airshaft whose disused and littered courtyard was patrolled by rats in search of edible rubbish and cats in search of edible rats, though two or three times during my tenancy the rats ganged up and managed to eat themselves a cat, nor was the ingestion of cousins and offspring unknown. The view was not much improved by glimpses of sad clerks in the back ends of offices around the shaft, or by what I could see of the goings-on in one of the ladies' rooms of S. Klein's On The Square cut-rate department store. Its big window, open in warm weather, was opposite my work table and occasionally there were some pretty good free-for-alls over package mix-ups or who was to get first go at a particular toilet stall, made more complex by the fact that some shoppers used the place for trying on skirts and blouses and things. But on the whole the ladies came across as just a quarrelsome aggregation of pale bulging flesh and I learned to ignore them most of the time, along with the cats and rats and filing clerks.

I achieved indifference also to the horrific mood music against which these scenes were enacted, the airshaft being a sounding box for all the racket of Union Square—the Square that S. Klein's was On and a zone of convergence for several bus lines and three subways. Even at three or four in the morning I could listen unheeding and unmoved, drifting toward sleep, to the amplified farting of great diesel engines, the squall of steel wheels on steel tracks, and frail piercing cries for succor rising up from murderous alleys here and there. To do so was a matter of functioning, of survival.

Though I remember that obliviousness clearly enough, I can't recapture its feel and indeed have a hard time these days believing it was really I who experienced it, so different was it from the sort of casual but constant observation of detail, the *noticingness*, of the rural life I've led for most of the past two decades. It would be simplistic to ascribe this contrast to some supposed superiority of a country existence

over the city kind, for I've known some dull and unobservant
rustics and have had some urban friends who missed very little
of what went on around them, from obscure marital tiffs on
subways to the fairyland glitter of mica in certain downtown
sidewalks. I've even liked certain cities well enough myself
and have lived awarely in them. But the country attitude I
mean is in some ways of another sort. It comes from having a
personal stake in the landscape that envelops you, in the various beasts and fowls and crops and objects it contains whose
ownership you claim, and in the activities of many wild things
that own themselves. To take stock of all this daily, to exercise surveillance, is about as much a requisite for survival as
was my Fifteenth Street indifference—survival for your chat-
tels alive or inert and therefore for you as a countryman. Because if you grow careless about what's happening on the
land, you stand a good chance of ending up broke and back
in town. In the country you *need* to notice things, and even
fairly fogheaded fellows like me attain a degree of alertness.

Bugs, for instance, are a part of human experience in almost any surroundings—flying up before one's feet in grass,
building ingenious nests under eaves or webs behind austere
computer panels, fluttering or zooming from tree to tree in
search of nectar or prey or love, expending their entrails on
windshields, scurrying beneath the water heater when the
kitchen light goes on, fiddling long sleepy heat-songs throughout afternoons in August, stinging or biting mammalian sur-
faces when such is their inclination. Yet in town only a few
species of them are ever much thought about, and most of
those few by suburbanites jealous of the wellbeing of the miniature farms they call yards. A countryman who runs his place
right, however, while he's unlikely to be an expert entomolo-
gist or even an adequate one, often has to be familiar with the
look and habits of dozens.

At a minimum, in my region, he knows greenbugs, grubs,

aphids, armyworms, ticks, fleas, lice, stinkbugs of three or four varieties, flies of six or eight, mosquitoes, various wasps and ants, crickets, grasshoppers, numerous kinds of spiders, and a host of specialized epicures like corn earworms, Colorado potato beetles, spotted and striped cucumber beetles, beeswax moths, peachtree borers, plum curculios, grape leaf-rollers, tomato hornworms, and squash bugs. Most matter to him as potential pests and enemies to be dealt with harshly, but others—predatory characters like ladybugs and mantises and spiders and some wasps, pollinators, soil-enriching earthworms, and so on—are friends and allies in his often doomed attempt to thwart rank nature's resolve to go her own sweet way.

He sees both sorts and their signs as he goes about his daily rounds, fleetingly for the most part but consciously enough that if they add up to a problem—clouds of hornflies tormenting his cattle, for instance, or a proliferation of cabbage loopers in the garden's lettuce—he can take some needed action. You may on occasion catch him doing queer things such as crumbling mud-dauber nests between his fingers to see what sort of anesthetized spiders have been stored there to feed the growing larvae. At least you could have caught me doing that last summer when the black widow spider population burgeoned alarmingly—which pleased the daubers greatly and set them off on a reproductive binge stoked with black widow meat, so that by autumn not only could I stick my hand into dark corners more or less without qualms, but the armatures of all unprotected electric motors were jammed with mud nests and among the materials composing my barn, adobe may have outweighed wood and sheet iron.

Bees make a botanist of their owner as he watches for blooms and nectar; in fact, the more varied the activities to which someone commits himself on and with the land, the keener his powers of observation are likely to become. Flat,

rich, monocultured country with wide expanses of wheat or milo or cotton and very little else requires no whetted perceptions on the part of its proprietor save in terms of soil conditions, weather, and a few sorts of weeds and insects. But an archaic type with a recalcitrant, rocky, up-and-down domain, who indulges his outworn notions of self-sufficiency by gardening, tending an orchard, sowing three or four field crops in their seasons, keeping poultry and bees and a milk cow, running goats and beef cattle and sheep, and even worrying over the fish in his stock ponds, needs to utilize such awareness as he can muster just about full-time, which I guess ought to add up to tension and neurosis but doesn't often seem to. More usually it comes out as the sort of equanimity that fitting in with one's world can give.

The real ones of this breed, those who have soaked up country habits and knowledge since childhood, grow older and fewer and amount perhaps to little in times geared to specialized agribusiness and the urban public it serves. Yet a good many of us latecomers and part-timers in the country admire the best of them and their ways, learning a little of what they know when we get a chance and imitating them as best we can in the privacy of our own terrain, like a movie-struck kid taking off Steve McQueen before the bathroom mirror. Having learned the hard way that ignorance vis-à-vis the landscape can cost dearly in dead or strayed or ailing animals and failed crops and whatnot, we pick up what we can from books and county agents and maybe evening ag-college courses, but this other kind of skill is seldom peddled in such places. It comes from living attentively on your own land and sometimes, when you're lucky, getting to watch someone intelligent who's spent a lifetime living that way.

If on a clear day in October there is a single dark puff of cloud on the northwestern horizon, such a man sees it within moments of coming outside (that swift eye-sweep of the sky that you find in all old rurals, even those ending their days in rest homes and wheeled onto a terrace for air) and gauges its probable meaning. Bouncing through a pasture in a pickup and passing a cow on her left side, he somehow discerns a wire cut on her right shoulder and checks it out for screw-worms, hemorrhage, or infection. At supper he may rise from the table in response to sounds that others have not heard, and go to the porch to learn where a pack of marauding dogs is running or a family of coyotes has its base. On a dusty path in the hills he can tell you, if asked, what creatures meek or fierce have trotted and slithered and shuffled there the night before. Distant columns of smoke have messages for him, as do neighbors' tractor sounds, shots, the urgent cries of jaybirds and crows, the alarm coughs of unseen deer, hill-side seeps, and the tinge of blooming sweetclover on damp evening air. All these things lodge in him and combine into understanding, for they are a part of his world, and so quite integrally is he.

Such honed vigilance is ancient, of course, tracing back to primitive tribesmen with eyes like falcons' and noses like setter dogs', and to the half-wild trappers and frontiersmen who felt out our continent for conquest not very long ago. In the best of their heirs it is by no means always economic in slant but adds up in part to "useless" wisdom, because having been led by circumstance into focusing good brains on natural phenomena instead of the civilized world's bright clutter and jabber and stink, they follow curiosity where it leads like academics, amassing knowledge for its own sake.

Many have read a good bit, and some have college degrees. I have one ranching friend, an Aggie ripe in years, who is al-ways good for a couple of hours' ruminative, expert discussion of wild vegetation in our area, utile or not, and long ago I knew a laconic old Hill Country native who had more in-formation on red ants than I've seen in books (admittedly I'm no deep reader on the subject), and admired them so much that he hated to disturb their beds in the course of farming and was hostile toward people who poisoned them. I liked him and respected his knowledge but was not converted, and to this day rather enjoy any chance to discommode the testy little bastards and get a measure of revenge for the many times one has climbed up my pants for a bite. Plowing is one way, though in certain years other small beings are upset by it too and express enough resentment for both themselves and the ants. Roaring along on your tractor you may find yourself suddenly in the middle of a towering cloud of bumblebees or the stubby yellowjackets that hive up by the thousands in burrows, and full many a crooked furrow or indeed a deserted machine has resulted from such attacks.

Days are when you see and touch things; nights are when other senses come most into play. Partly for this reason I don't much like closed bedrooms and really prefer sleeping on a screened porch, as I used to do all year long till a couple of arctic winters in a row chased me back inside. Ensconced on a porch with your head sticking out of the covers and only a film of wire gauze between you and the vast starred blackness outside, you're in tune with the night, or at any rate as much in tune with it as your perceptions will let you be.

The far-off rising groan of big Macks and Whites as they shift to low gear on the hills of U.S. 67 means a drift of air from the southeast, and means also that its Gulf moisture may give the region a shot at wanted rain within the next few days. A standard whiff of polecat, not unpleasant, tells you only that one is foraging somewhere, but a stouter whang indicates he may be at your hives again, scrabbling with his claws at the entrance to bring the bees out in their dudgeon, then gobbling them up with stings for piquant seasoning. Cows with milk-taut bags bawl urgently for roving offspring, and if one hungry answer comes from a wrong direction and lasts too long and sounds a trifle desperate, you know a calf has blundered through a fence and you'll have to do something about it in the morning. Coyotes on the hill to the east yap and wail and trill in sudden chorus for a minute or so to establish hunting contact or possibly just for love of music, then go silent; owls talk; a cottontail shrieks as something (what?) grabs it; a being unknown says hark-o-hark-hark in the west. A dog's voice goes softly woo-woo in the distance and you know that the Edwards kid is out with his mongrel "silent trailer" again and they've treed something, which leads you into reflection on the high pelt prices that have all furred varmints under siege. Hens on a liveoak branch beside the house stir and mutter in sleep; Leghorns rescued by your daughter from the biology lab at school, they grew up as gentle pets and refuse to roost in the barn where the rape-minded gamecock and his combative harem of one hold sway. The sheep dog snores and snuffles on the concrete floor beside your bed, but wakes to growl in his throat at something, maybe old Woo-woo....

Nights are thus very rich, right on into that zone of fading consciousness where real noises and smells blend with dozing illusion, and afterward too for that matter, since the sleep of attunement is light, if sound, and doesn't much mind interruption. I remember once having a dream in which a buzzing, clucking, angry, continuous voice took on the shape of whirl-pooling points of light, then waking and going out into frozen moon-glow to find that Blue, our only dog then, had treed a ringtail in a hackberry beside the garden, and I didn't resent the waking or the cold or the effort since they served to teach me the exact origin of that sound I'd heard before in ignorance, thinking it was probably coons. But I confess it may take a special sort of picayunish concern with natural things to see the matter so.

Picayunish or not, it is a sort of concern—sometimes practical, sometimes not—that I share with a lot of other people out beyond the cities' rims. And if it is a far far cry from being able to slumber rosily through the pandemonic nightly din of Union Square and to glance with unseeing eyes at the antics of fat ladies squabbling half-clad in a restroom, I guess what the difference really has to do with is belonging. What it may show is that when you're somewhere you don't especially want to be and don't belong, you tend to wall yourself off from sentience like a hibernating bear, whereas in surroundings that you care for and have chosen, you use eyes, ears, nose, tastebuds, and whatever other aids you can muster for reception. You notice. And, noticing, you live.

Weather
Between East and West

Cold, the physics textbooks used to claim and probably still do, is merely an absence of heat and thus doesn't really exist. I can accept this idea on faith, as one accepts so many dicta these days right up to the notion of black holes in space, but in practical ways I've never been able to make much sense out of it. The malevolence of a January day when a sleet-flecked fourteen-degree wind from out of the Canadian Arctic is buffeting my numbed self, as I lurch zombielike except for curses about my daily rural tasks, doesn't strike me as the absence of anything, really, but as the presence of itself. So does a handful of ice cubes making bell music against the sides of a glass of some pleasant stimulant on a sunbaked August afternoon.

Similarly, I guess it could be said that dryness is just a shortage of wetness, but it too has stout identity when rain refuses to fall, grasses and crops go dormant or die, and planted seeds won't sprout. And it is these four things and their interplay—heat, cold, moisture, drouth—that make up most of what we call weather, wherever we happen to live. On occasion wind gets into it powerfully too, of course, as do things like mountains, oceans, latitudes, and barometric highs and lows, but most of the time these serve as mere determinants of the amount and frequency and form in which any given place receives the four basics.

In our time and our part of the world, a good proportion of people are more or less divorced from worry over weather, except as it relates to outdoor pleasures like golf and water-skiing. Their agricultural impulse, if any, is largely limited to lawns and shrubs that can be kept alive with cheap plentiful hydrant water if clouds fail to do the job; the houses they live in and the buildings where they work are engineered to provide those year-round temperatures and humidities most agreeable to lightly decked, sedentary human torsos. A lawyer-philosopher friend of mine maintains that they're best for the psyche and brain as well, and cites Plato's cave, which he insists remained a steady seventy-two degrees Fahrenheit in all seasons, just as his own home and office do. Since Plato as I recall didn't live in the cave but only used it as metaphor, I don't know what this would prove if true, but there it is.

What is certain is that our cities have grown dependent on such ameliorations, and if the energy shortage ever gets bad enough that airconditioners die en masse, a jaundiced non-cave dweller expects that the cloud of dust raised by Wisconsinites and upper New York Staters and other boreal DP's stampeding out of the Sun Belt for home will very likely rival the one caused by Krakatoa when it blew in 1883. Weather will matter once more in towns and cities then, and those of us who grew up in urban Texas before cooling equipment prevailed can vouch that what will matter most down here is summer heat, especially in the sort of houses and office buildings that have become the rule.

Nearly all kinds of weather still matter out in the sticks, even to people who live in cooled, centrally heated homes and own tractors and pickups whose cabs are equivalently de-weatherized. For despite such little technological havens, much of what countrymen have to do is still in the full outdoors, and their heaviest concerns—the growth and wellbeing of crops and grasses and beasts—are tied to the climate's vagaries during whatever season. There is no way they can get around thinking about the weather; it is integral to their context and their being. So they still study it, talk at length about it, predict what it will do, and brood when it turns out "wrong" for their purposes.

These purposes being often divergent, what weather is "right" at a specific time and place can be a relative question. A July cloudburst that fills shrinking stock ponds with water and starts pasture grass to shooting up green and tender and swells cattlemen's hearts with satisfaction may enrage a fellow whose nearly ripe bottomland milo needs no water and has just been expensively sprayed against bugs. Peanut farmers in my neighborhood dislike fall rains, welcomed by everyone else, because they can delay harvest and make undug goobers go moldy in the ground. Or an unrelieved eight weeks of damp bitter cold in late winter and what ought to be early spring, anathema to farmers who want to get started plowing and planting and to stockmen who have to shell out cash for extra feed and catch flu while doling it out to their animals, may be viewed as a special boon by a purveyor of firewood or propane or a man with a commercial peach orchard, who knows such weather will ensure the long dormancy that his trees require to make a good crop in summer. And since orchardist and woodcutter and stockman and farmer may not only be neighbors but indeed at times may inhabit the same denim jacket, the wishes that hover in the air at such times are so opposed that should some beneficent force chance to be listening, he might well wonder wherein beneficence lies. An interesting example of this sort of thing was an old lady's statement I overheard one day in April when I picked up the telephone to make an urgent call, and found as often that the party line was occupied. "I wish," she said in a cracked, slow, musing voice that gave promise the two of them would be maundering on for at least another half-hour, "it would rain real hard on my radishes and onions but not on my crowder peas."

Climatically as well as culturally, Texas is a transitional region between East and West. The ninety-eighth meridian, viewed by the late Walter Prescott Webb as the essential boundary between the two, bisects the state a little east of center, and wavering back and forth across this meridian in rough coincidence with it is another imaginary but meaningful line, the thirty-inch isohyet of average annual rainfall. In these latitudes, generally speaking, ordinary Eastern-style agriculture dependent on rain is feasible with thirty inches or more of moisture per year, i.e., to the east of the line, whereas less means a rural economy based more on range stock-raising, with farming restricted to drouth-resistant grasslike crops such as wheat and the grain sorghums, except in zones where water from rivers or reservoirs or underground deposits can be tapped for irrigation.

Webb defined these things for us, but he based his definition on the tough experience of hordes of farmers, including his own father, who during the closing decades of the nineteenth century and the early ones of the twentieth ventured out beyond thirty inches to try to raise Eastern cash crops, mainly cotton, on homestead-sized tracts of unirrigated land. Occasional abnormally wet years kept hope alive for a good while, and some farmers are still making the effort, usually with more sophisticated techniques and on a larger scale. But most small-timers gave up the sweaty fight during the Dust Bowl years of the Thirties, if not before. Normality in the long run had prevailed and beaten them down.

Normality being drouth, and drouth being not only a probability west of ninety-eight but a constant possibility well to its east also. Nature deals less in lines than in zones, and conditions in areas of transition are fragile because they're so easily altered from year to year by small variations in things like moisture, which would make little practical difference to people in, say, the damp forests near the Louisiana line. If in some relatively wet years the thirty-inch rainfall line strays a good way west of ninety-eight, gladdening hardbitten survivors in near West Texas, in others it will unpredictably move eastward and strew agricultural ruination up and down the rich Blackland Prairies and the Post Oak Belt.

If you add to this the fact that in western reaches of this transition zone and beyond it, range grasses may often not get enough precipitation to feed the cattle that depend on them and can't migrate elsewhere as the buffalo used to do at such times, what you end up with is a very large hunk of Texas, a strip hundreds of miles wide running down the middle of the state, where worry over drouth is a basic part of rural human existence. Drouth has helped shape us Texans as a people, if we still are one in such mixing-bowl times as these, and it keeps on shaping hell out of those of us who have anything to do with the land. It lurks and skulks on the outskirts of the lushest seasons; whenever a few weeks go by without rain some people start crying dry doom, and in the nature of things they sometimes have to be right.

In one or another part of the state, in fact, they're likely to be right at almost any time, and in my own part of it they're right right now, and have been for nearly a year and a half. It is early November as I write this, and since a year ago last May my place, which lies about ten miles east of the ninety-eighth meridian in North Central Texas, has not received any generous rain, the kind that falls in quantity and is followed not by dry winds and bright sun that snatch it back into the atmosphere but rather by cloudy weather and more rain to drive moisture into the root zone of grasses and crops and trees and down through the subsoil to bedrock, along which it percolates to the bases of dirt bluffs along watercourses and emerges as cool seep springs.

Our creek, normally a good one for this area, is dry and has been so for months except when a transient storm has set it to trickling for a day or so, or maybe as much as a week. You can dig a four-foot cornerpost hole, and a clod from its bottom, if you crumble it in your hand, will turn to dust. Many stock ponds have shrunk to puddles or cracked dry mud. Some brushy plants and even oaks in gravelly places are dead; expensive exotic grasses sowed in spring by neighbors of mine came up with May showers and then died too. We got no surplus honey from the bees this summer, since even those plants that managed to bloom yielded little nectar, and like many others in the region I've cut my little herd of cows to half its usual size—fortunately selling the culls in a favorable market, for much of the cash they brought will have to go into feed for the survivors this winter, which looks fair to be a sort of Mongolian one with big dry frigid winds that raise dust to sting your face.

It's a blessing at such times to be in part a dilettante, not heavily dependent on the climate's quirks for a living, but others whom I know and care about are dependent, cattlemen and farmers both. Not far away men who raise peanuts on sandy land are hoping barely to make back, from a fractional crop, the cost of their seed and fertilizer and the payments on the heavy costly equipment they use, but in their heads they're rehearsing eloquence to use on creditors if they don't.

Drouth. You don't have to be a full believer in the theory of twenty-two-year cycles, based on sunspot patterns, to feel a certain sick quiver of your insides when you note that it's only twenty-one since the big bad one of the Fifties ended, so that another year or so of the same could well be looming ahead. Nor do you have to be a fundamentally sour-natured fellow to blaspheme with sincerity when you wake up in the morning and gaze out at yet another clear sky full of stars, portending another fine day. It is part of the shaping I mentioned.

When the weather around here is not too dry, it is sometimes awful in other ways, for our moisture, when it does come, takes the form of gentle soaking rain only on occasion. High winds and hail and lightning and flooding are fascinating conversational fodder, and when two or more countrymen get on such subjects the tales multiply like combat anecdotes among a beery group of veterans of Guadalcanal or the Bulge. I am thus afflicted myself, but also aware of the danger of longwindedness inherent in such excursions. . . . Here, let me merely note the time when lightning whacked our tin barn. I was watching from the front porch of the house, and staggered over against sweeping sheets of rain to see if the bolt had started a fire. It hadn't, though it had made junk out of the structure's wiring system, and some twenty-five Spanish goats that had taken refuge under the front overhang were lying about in various contorted positions, some groaning in human tones and others knocked out cold. The billy, a black ill-smelling specimen known as Martin Shockley, was lying on his back with the points of his wide horns stuck in the ground, his four legs in the air, and a peaceful look on his face. All recovered, but they stayed paranoid concerning that place of shelter for months afterward, refusing at first to come there even for corn or oats.

Or consider, if I may allow myself just one more anecdote, our sole close tornado, a small one that passed through the yard of the old farmhouse near Fort Worth that we leased and lived in when first married. It exploded our stone garage, plucked my canoe from the rafters to deposit it unharmed high up in the angle-iron underpinnings of a water tower seventy-five feet away, defeathered and destroyed some bantams, made a great deal of noise, but somehow missed the house. I was away, and when a neighbor hurried over just afterward to see how my wife had fared, she met him at the door. "I'm fine," she said in a firm clear voice. "It didn't really bother me at all."

"Yes, ma'am," said the neighbor. "Maybe you better let me hold that baby a minute." Said infant having gone purple from near-strangulation as it dangled from the crook of her arm by its neck.

It used to be that nearly all country homes in these parts of Texas, even stark boxing-plank shacks, had a storm cellar dug nearby where the family would repair when the sky grew dark and the clouds turned sulphur-green, and some clans had a reputation for "going to the cellar" at the slightest provocation. Few are being built these days, though the early Sixties with their emphasis on fallout shelters spawned a few fancy specimens on ranches of the well-to-do, and a good many of the rest of us who live out where approaching storms are visible from afar, in all their glory and frightfulness, have occasion every year or two or three to wish we had been provident enough to excavate one too. But then the storm passes, and we fall back on the comforting reflection that if there were very much chance of a tornado hitting any given spot there wouldn't be any old houses left in the region.

This climate's propensity toward drouth and violence has prevented even the brashest Chambers of Commerce from getting very lyrical about it. But, perhaps a bit inconsistently, I'd like to set down my own opinion that except for those things, it really isn't too bad. You only need to have lived a couple of years or so in places where snow and cold feet last for six months each year, to appreciate the fact that our own rhythmic winters, with warmish damp Gulf air pushing up time and again, and time and again being shoved back south by cold fronts from the north, are very mild stuff, even if the two rough ones just behind us did give us a taste of what Yankees have to take for granted year after year. April and May can be magnificent with birdsong and wildflowers and greenery gone crazy, and if good rains come in late August or September, as they often do, early fall can be a sort of verdant second spring before frosts turn it red and blue and yellow and crisp. Furthermore, at the risk of stirring up urban newcomers and people like my legal crony who dwells with Herr Doktor Fahrenheit at the back end of Plato's cave, I will note that even our vaunted summer heat is not all that hard to take if you have to take it, at least not in the country. For the most part it isn't humid heat; breezes do blow; nights, away from sun-soaked radiant city pavements, are nearly always cool for sleeping; and when the unrelenting hundred-degree-plus days start, usually in July, the body makes one of those shifts of attunement of which it is capable, and within a short period (longer, I concede, as the body in question accumulates years and a thicker trunk) such days are simply the way things are. One functions, as does the land if it's given half a chance.

. . .

Obviously people dependent on weather need any prior knowledge they can get hold of concerning what the weather is likely to do. Up till not very long ago a goodly part of traditional rustic wisdom consisted of saws and maxims on the subject, and in most neighborhoods certain individuals were acknowledged to have superior talent in prediction, reading barometric pressures through skin or sinuses or old wounds and interpreting clouds and the veerings of wind as seers once did chicken guts, or often a bit more usefully. Weather patterns being regional in character, the maxims varied with geography, so that the "red sky at night" that promised clear days ahead in one place might be viewed in another as a promise that all hell was getting ready to break loose.

Seafaring communities, where a bad weather guess could get you drowned, were especially fertile in this sort of lore. On one Mediterranean island where I spent most of a year a quarter-century ago and had a little sailboat, there existed a solid array of homely jingles in the local dialect of Catalan, most of them translatable to Spanish without a loss of rhyme, that detailed prospects for the weather and navigation as manifested in various winds and temperatures and cloud formations. They had probably been bandied there in one form or another since the Romans had run the place, and they worked. One that I remember went, *Al norte joven o al sur viejo, no te fíes el pellejo*—don't trust your hide to a young north wind or an old one from the south—and once when I flouted it and sailed forth with a French lady companion in a fresh pleasant northerly breeze, we got a thorough wetting and were lucky not to have gotten worse.

Some weather lore, especially over here where we haven't had since the Romans to distill it down to accuracy, seems to be based on wishful thinking—wishful in terms of wanting to believe either that one *can* predict the weather good or bad, or that desirable weather is really on its way. I used to have a country neighbor who during drouths would inevitably, when he saw a white rim of cloudiness on the eastern horizon, prognosticate a gully-washer, a clod-melter, a frog-strangler within the week. He claimed to have had it in childhood from a grandfather—and might, I sometimes thought, have garbled it a bit while growing up, or maybe his ancestor had picked it up in Tennessee or somewhere else besides Texas. When rain failed to come he would forget or ignore having foretold it, but out of eighteen or twenty such predictions that I heard him make over a period of years, sheer mathematics caused rain to show up a couple of times, whereupon he had himself a gloat. "Hot Chihuahua!" he said once when all my fence watergaps on the creek and its branches had been washed out by the runoff from a five-inch slosher, and his own hay crop had been flattened and chewed ragged by the attendant hail. "I told you Granddaddy knowed how things worked."

But many folksy beliefs do have some connection with what's happening in the realm of weather, and even sometimes with what's going to happen. I haven't had occasion to check out what the belly hair of certain mammals, the structure of wasp nests, the number and shape of mesquite pods, the depth of tortoises' burrows, and other such things may have to do with the severity of a coming winter, but I don't feel like sneering at them either, at least if they involve regional flora and fauna rather than exotics like the groundhog. In my own little bailiwick I've been convinced of at least the partial and poetic accuracy of some native convictions, such as the one that the arrival of slate-colored juncos means that snow is in the offing. Called "snowbirds" locally for this reason, these trim little finches don't really arrive on such occasions, for they're thick if secretive in our cedarbrakes and brush piles throughout the cold months. But during a spell of quiet cloudy weather of the kind that often presages a midwinter front and possible snow, they do lose some of their habitual shyness and are seen in small flocks around yards and corrals, gobbling up all the seeds and spilled grain and other fuel they can find against a probable spell of lean pickings.

There is a good bit of accuracy too in old-timers' belief that the best rains in our region come out of the southwest, which at first blush seems improbable because that's the direction of the driest parts of Texas and Mexico. With the old ones the theory was based on long observation, but it tallies with the fact that our main shots at helpful moisture come during spring and fall when cold fronts, arriving most often from somewhere in the compass pie-slice between slightly north of west and slightly west of north, butt heads with wet Gulf or Pacific air and set off storms. The storms, after forming, generally move along rather slowly in a northeasterly direction, parallel to the triggering front rather than with it. Hence if you see a thunderhead or a squall line of them to your approximate southwest you do stand a fair chance of getting some rain, whereas if it shows up in some other quadrant you'll more than likely have to watch it go elsewhere, wetting other people's pastures and fields. The rule doesn't always work, especially for typical summer thunderstorms, which can shape up individually or in big "cells" out of unstable air and moisture in an otherwise clear sky, then zigzag about the landscape in just about any direction they fancy, defying all theories and maxims that I've heard. There is thus a larger component of frustration in watching one of these slide by only a couple of miles away, flashing and grumbling atop its thick column of rain, when with luck it might have caught you square and added up to a thousand bales or so of Sudan hay for winter.

Frustration is also a common result of paying too much attention to the workings of modern meteorology, as practically all of us country types do. Thorough and informed television weather reports and forecasts, with maps and radar screens and those other wonders that have supplanted aching hip joints and hoary jingles as sources of prediction, are in my estimation one of the more bearable elements of progress, if you set aside a tendency in most forecasters to pander to a mass urban audience by bemoaning weekend rain, or praising the chances for lovely dry weather when lousy wet weather is what the land is craving. Even the best of these soothsayers, though, can deal only in probabilities, and probabilities as many a crap-shooter knows to his sorrow are nasty, tricky things. If you learn from the lips of Harold Taft of Channel 5 in Fort Worth, my own special hero among TV characters, that prospects are just right for a major and badly needed downpour, and then the downpour doesn't eventuate for reasons that may ultimately have to do with the way winds are playing around among the peaks of the Himalayas, you experience more than just plain workaday disappointment and indeed may say some ugly things about hero Harold, not really meaning them. You'd have been much better off not watching his neat, swirl-marked, shaded maps or his satellite photos, not knowing that science was on your side, not getting your hopes up.

Yet hope and worry about the weather have always been the lot of countrymen, and I doubt this will change much even in the unlikely event that meteorology becomes an exact science, making Harold and his counterparts heroes every time. For the truth is that doubt and worry and hope about large external forces are something we are geared for, and probably need, and sometimes even enjoy. I wouldn't swap the white and dark-blue magnificence and promise and threat of a sixty-thousand-foot-tall thunderhead on the southwestern horizon in May for two dozen of Plato's caves. I wouldn't even swap this damned drouth.

Coronado's Stepchildren

The last really obsessed treasure-hunter in our area died two or three years ago at a reasonably advanced age, never having found any of what he was looking for as far as I've heard, but having apparently enjoyed the quest all the way. I hardly knew him except by sight, for I'm not a native and obsessed people are hard to approach from outside the framework that produced them. He came around once, alighting from a lop-sided old black pickup and fixing me with small close-set black eyes on either side of a large pitted nose as we traded names and handshakes. Then he scuffed the toe of one work shoe in the gravel for a moment and announced that the Spanish had dug long galleries in a soft stratum of my hills

179

across the creek and after filling them with silver bullion had plugged the entries and gone away, never to return.

I said, "I didn't think there were any Spanish here in the first place, this far north. The Comanches . . ."

"Hell yes, the Comanches," he said. "That's why they left, them Spaniards. Couldn't stick around here, and later on they couldn't come back. Hit weren't only the Indians but the Meskin Revolution too."

"Yes," I said. "How'd you find out about it?"

Small dark eyes gone darker with secrecy: "I know lots of things they don't nobody else know."

I, with diplomacy that seemed to be needed: "I bet you do."

"Shit, I know where they's a great big old slab of ledge rock, weighs maybe two ton, never been moved. And on the bottom side they's stuff carved in that rock. They's an owl, and a wolf, and a woman. And she's blonde-headed and she's got *square titties*."

"If it's never been moved, how'd you ever . . ."

But that was an overstep, and the secrecy and suspicion moved over his whole thin, seamed face. "Yeah," he said, and with a disgusted sort of grumble got back in the pickup and drove off.

Other landowners seized his drift less skeptically, and some of them still have grubby documents that attest to agreements to split treasure found on such and such premises at a rate of fifty-fifty betwixt owner of said premises and finder of said treasure. There is a very noble hole a few miles from my place, six feet in diameter and fifteen deep through solid limestone, with a tunnel taking off horizontally from the bottom God knows how far, which this same fellow and an aging farmer totally hooked on his visions dug with picks and crowbars and dynamite, expecting to intersect some dream-certified chamber stuffed full of precious metals. The project collapsed when the farmer did likewise and was hauled off to an institution, but his source of inspiration just started another dig elsewhere. I was somehow rather shocked when I wandered over from the county road not long ago to inspect that hole again, and found that a new owner has been using it for garbage disposal.

Spanish galleries aside, our hilly neighborhood is an improbable sort of place to be looking for such loot. In the first place its geology is sedimentary, with nearly level layers of limestone lying on top of one another down to considerable depths, interrupted here and there by flat beds of shale and clay and water-bearing sand, with no trace of the sort of volcanic activity that forces ores precious or otherwise up within men's greedy reach. Hence, with little chance of lost mines and bullion such as J. Frank Dobie wrote about in *Coronado's Children* and elsewhere, legends and lore about treasure hereabouts are likely to tell of human hoardings squirreled away somewhere for posterity to find. But here one confronts the coldwater fact that human wealth has never been very probable around these parts, either. Though the country itself was more productive when virgin a century and more ago, it wasn't even then the sort of land where surplus riches abounded to the point that their concealment was very often required. Nor in the millennia before white settlement were there any inhabitants equivalent in material glory to Aztecs, Incas, Egyptians, or those fierce Scythian tribesmen of the Old World who buried kings and chieftains with heaped precious figurines and ornaments. There were only Tonkawas and other tough, impoverished, hunting-and-gathering Indians, eking out a living from mussels and roots and game and berries and decorating themselves alive or dead, if at all, with bits of shell and bone and animal fangs.

Certainly an occasional jar of silver dollars or paper money must have been secreted in a post hole or mortared beneath some limestone hearth after a good cotton crop or a small inheritance or the sale of a herd of cows, and I suppose it is on such events, rumored and exaggerated in families and crossroads communities, that most of such lore as we have had is based. It is fading now as the old natives die off and their progeny move away to seek another sort of treasure at construction projects and auto assembly plants, and it was seldom bruited widely, since those who knew about such things generally had some hope of unearthing the trove for themselves. But it existed, and if you spent any time nosing about in abandoned country houses, as I used to in my more unfettered days, you would sometimes find clear traces not of loot but at least of somebody else's search for it.

I set down a tale in a book once about a land deal in this region in which the seller reserved ownership of an old shack where a bachelor uncle of his had lived for many years and died. It wasn't much of a structure but the land's buyer, a friend of mine, thought that maybe it had sentimental value for the old fellow and he was going to move it elsewhere. Not bloody likely. He camped there and dismantled it plank by plank and stone by stone, and when he was done he went away and left the whole mess lying on the ground. He had been looking for something whose existence was vouched for in family talk, though what it was and whether he found it, none of us ever learned.

Another legend attached to the sad little house occupied by a pair of spinsters up until the time of their deaths in the Forties. They were all that was left of a family that had earlier been rich in local terms, with ten or twelve sections of land. But that had all been squandered by their father and brothers, and the old ladies finished out their lives on a small barren corner of those once extensive holdings. One of them was paralyzed in the legs and the other maneuvered her from bed to chair or table or elsewhere by grasping her waist from behind and dragging her about the house; the heels of her shoes, it is said, were worn quite round by this procedure. Neighbors worked the pair's little rocky fields on shares and they managed to live on that and a tiny bit of county dole money, and were supposed to have thousands of dollars hidden away somewhere. The house was blown to pieces by a tornado not long after they died, within a few months of each other, but people used to go there and dig, some of the latter searchers bringing metal detectors and other such paraphernalia. One difficulty in taking it seriously lay in the obvious fact, commented on by a neighbor, that if they'd had any money at all, "you know damn well they'd of dug out enough to buy a wheel chair. Ain't nobody all that tight."

I guess it's not really a paradox, though, that treasure legends seem to have flourished best in poor or desert places. For the people in such places need more acutely than anyone else to believe in the possibility of windfall things that might suddenly and drastically alleviate their lot. Thus the champion treasure-believers of our continent are probably northern Mexicans and the rural Latins of Texas and the rest of the Southwest who are descended from them. And their lore in this as in other things tends to be much richer than its Anglo equivalent.

I knew an old Mexican midwife living in a little South Texas town who had second sight and liked to tell stories about these matters with waving, carving hands and with flashings and squintings and widenings of her very blue eyes. (Another story, those eyes: the Canary Islands father shot by revolutionists and the ranch-hand husband she married at fifteen because he threatened to knife her if she didn't, and the rest . . .) She and her husband when young had worked for a German rancher, a miser beyond compare. One night—the eve of some specific saint's day, but I forget which one—when she went out of their shack for something, she saw beneath a pear tree in the German's yard a flickering flame like that of a candle, but blue. When she went closer it disappeared, but when she returned to her doorway and looked back toward the tree, the flame was there again. Next morning she mentioned it to the rancher and he paled (she did too when telling of it, somehow) and said with anger Nein, nein, it could not be, do not talk about it. And the day after *that* there was a big hole under the pear tree, with the imprint still in it of a jug or some other round container that had been removed. Two weeks later, saying there was not enough work to be done even though sheep-shearing was coming up, the German fired them.

Which led to more stories as Grandma Elizondo's tales were wont to do, and I wish I'd written some down instead of having to rely on hazy recollection now. She was a power in the town, whose population was mainly Latin and Teutonic and heavily Catholic, and once when a new priest made some motions toward ethnically segregated seating in the church she showed up at his house. "Come in, Mrs. Elizondo, come in," he said.

"I can't," said Grandma. "I stink." Which finished off that particular bit of trouble.

Another pear tree story has little to do with treasure, but does illustrate the continuing sense of ownership that country people can have about old family places even after they've been sold into strangers' hands. The tree in question was an old one and large, with juicy sweet fruit, possessing an immunity to the fire blight that attacks nearly all good pear trees in Texas. The place it stood on lay lost back in the cedar of our hills, with no public roads passing by to bring in drifters. An observant city landowner, having bought that land and tacked it onto his adjoining ranch, noticed the tree loaded with green fruit in the first summer of his ownership, but when he came back in autumn he found it already stripped, with only a few cull pears still hanging yellow on the branches or lying on the ground. The next year the same thing happened, so the third year he kept a close watch weekend by weekend, and when most of the fruit was ripe he picked it for himself, feeling a certain moral glee in the four or five bushels he got.

And the next fall after that, when he went to look, the tree had been chopped down.

Tobacco Without Smoke I:
Dippers

Snuff, the powdered form of tobacco, is not a centrally important commodity these days. On this side of the Atlantic those people to whom it does still matter are found for the most part in our Southern states, and they are mainly country and village traditionalists with a notable degree of built-in resistance to swinging, changing, urban ways. Swinging, changing urbans in their turn, at least those who are even aware of snuff's existence, tend to see it as broadly comic, and a reference to it in such company is nearly always good for a general cackling laugh. For humor, as we are told, is rooted in a sense of superiority, and "dipping"—the taking of snuff by mouth in Southern country style—is a fairly easy thing to feel superior to, for reasons that will perhaps emerge.

At its social peak snuff was not dipped but snuffed, applied to the nasal mucosa by inhalation, and if you'd laughed at some of its users you might not have laughed again on this side of the dueling ground. During two or three centuries in most civilized countries, including some unlikely ones such as China, snuffing was the most patrician way of using tobacco, though the other ways persisted strongly and it was perhaps an American practitioner of one of them who sang somewhat sardonically:

> *Some it chew, some it smoke,*
> *Some it up their nose do poke.*

But nasal snuffing fell from style in this country before the Civil War and has never been widely revived. The uproar about cigarette smoking that followed the Surgeon General's famous pronouncement of a few years back did inspire certain entrepreneurs to attempt the reintroduction of European high-grade snuff to these shores for such use, most American sorts intended for oral application being far too rank and strong for the nose. Promotional campaigns were launched which bore down cannily on snuffing lore from the eighteenth century, a halcyon time for "the great sternutatory," as someone called it, when Beau Brummell and other arbiters prescribed how jeweled boxes should be held while taking a perfumed pinch and looked down their aquiline snuff-laden noses at vulgarians who smoked. (The vulgarians, naturally, reciprocated in kind: one germane passage in a roguish and readable old book called *Ned Ward's London* describes the entrance of some dandies into a tavern where the author and his friends sit puffing clay pipes, and notes with plebeian glee the dandies' disgust with the fumes and their manner of taking out "snush boxes" and conveying the contents to their nostrils.) Great names redolent of that era were invoked in the names of brands and scented flavors: Sarah Siddons, Dean Swift, Dr. Johnson. . . . However, this praiseworthy if rather snooty effort to bypass the contemporary connotations of snuff in the U.S., where too many upwardly mobile individuals have clear but uneasy recollection of a country-bred grandmother sucking on a fat lipful of Tube Rose Sweet while at ease in her rocking chair, seems not to have had great lasting impact except among a scattering of experimenters like me.

The only lingering American tradition of nasal snuffing that I've run across involved West Virginia lumberjacks of a generation or so ago, but a good many people from recently immigrated families have known older relatives who it up their nose did poke, for in certain European areas and social groups the habit is still entrenched. The brand of snuff that I like best for occasional use, unscented and stout but smooth, is manufactured in Belfast by the "scotch" process (meaning "scorch," but that is a longish tale in itself) and kept in stock by a Washington, D.C., tobacconist for the convenience of some Irish-born priests who will deign to sniff no other. I'm told the snuffboxes in the U.S. Senate chambers are kept full as long practice prescribes but are seldom used except by an occasional member with a bad foggy hangover, which would indicate that the snuff therein, patriotically, is American, for while it may be rank its jolt when inhaled is guaranteed to wake you up.

Old snuffing anecdotes abound but are interesting, I suppose, for the most part only to snuffers. One that somehow has poignance for me concerns Charles Lamb's genteel but eccentric sister Mary, who when making a round of social calls always carried several empty snuffboxes in her reticule, and if left alone for a few minutes in a parlor would surreptitiously load one full from her hostess's mantel box.

Snuffing in comparison to other forms of tobacco use has a fairly immediate effect—you can get dizzy on it, after abstention—that is more marked than the gentle euphoria induced by chewing or dipping, but not nearly as strong as the tingle and glow of a great double lungful of cigarette smoke. It gives you the full savor of good tobacco with or without accompanying perfume, affords an excuse to collect pretty snuffboxes and patterned dark snuffing handkerchiefs, and is on the whole a very pleasant and satisfying practice if you don't mind a bit of sneezing now and then and the upraised eyebrows of people around you. It inflicts no "tar" upon the system and when performed correctly (a short sharp sniff into each nostril is the ticket) doesn't reach your lungs, and I expect it will be a long long while before the Surgeon General or anyone else will be able to accumulate enough statistics to prove definitely that it's bad for your health, as it no doubt is. Former ages were divided on this point, some sour medicos claiming it did loathsome things to the noses of excessive users, but in general it was thought therapeutic. My own experience indicates that it does help sinus trouble but on the other hand intensifies hay fever.

Of snuff that is taken country style, i.e. in the mouth, the wet, coarsely ground, highly popular sort often called "snoose" has been classified by me and certain other scholars and musers in the field, after much thought and heated consultation, as really a form of chewing tobacco, and I'll deal with it at length when I get to that topic. Dry snuff, the true light-brown powder cherished by many generations of rural Southerners—white, black, male, female, young, old—is found on the shelves of country and small-town stores in little cylindrical friction-top cans, fine when empty for storing small childhood treasures, and in larger glass containers. It is of two main sorts, sweet and salty, and though, as is well known, tradition is going to hell in a handbasket these days, mild sweet snuff used to be favored chiefly by women and beginners while adult males leaned to the stronger salty kind, with vehement loyalty to one brand or another.

A friend of mine grew up in the East Texas woods and during adolescence worked in his family's small sawmill when not in school. Among the other workers, mainly black, was one huge fellow who used to say in toast from time to time, as he poised a heaping tin lid of fresh brown dust before his lip preparatory to dumping it within: "That Mist' Levi Garrett, he the greatest inventor they *ever* was!" Lots of dippers still agree, and when you hear the term Levi in some sections it still doesn't usually mean jeans. But Levi's relative W. E. Garrett had and has many adherents too, along with Honest, Tube Rose, Rooster, Dental, and some other brands, though conglomerate octopi have been at work and the list is not nearly as long as it was.

Men who dip are still fairly common in rural Texas, especially in the eastern parts; the habit is a powerful one, it is said, much harder to break than cigarettes. But the greater part of them, an observer and merely tentative dipper thinks to discern, are of those generations that did their growing up before the Second World War, for though of late there has been a solid increase in tobacco chewing, younger recruits have not been flocking to the banner of snuff, which sadly lacks social cachet. In fact, in modern times snuff has been held in lower esteem, by what my mother used to call "nice people," than any other form of tobacco use. Why this should be so is a bit moot, though not very. In some part, I suspect, it's based on an old urban tendency to look down on specifically rural ways, and partly too on a spookiness about their origins in many ex-rural townsmen who are trying hard to be "nice" themselves. But it would be very rash to get oversociological about all this and to gloss over the hard central fact, lamentable but known to all with eyes, that an occasional carefree dipper can be a truly gross and repellent sight.

Slogans, as we wearily know, are the soul of salesmanship, and the older generation of advertising men used to recite to each other one example which had brought great success to, I believe, a young cigar company touting the superiority of its machine-made product over the traditional handcrafted sort stuck together with human saliva: "Spit is a horrid word." It is widely considered to be a fairly horrid substance as well, especially when brown. You can dip or chew with little if any concomitant expectoration, as many secret users do, by simply tucking a small pinch of snuff or a pea-sized lump of tobacco between your cheek and lower gum. But for many other addicts, full hearty satisfaction demands larger quantities than that, and while even a fair-sized chew of tobacco will "settle down" after a time and require no further spitting, snuff is unfortunately different. Its finely particulate consistency means that a real wad steadily releases into the mouth a flow of potent juice that nobody without a ceramic stomach can swallow. Hence a periodic patooie is inevitable—or more accurately, with snuff, a thin and dark-amber squirt. Some dippers who work outdoors alone or in masculine company, where niceties are not crucial, can pack in heroic amounts at a time and are often what is known as "front-lippers"— insouciant fellows who don't bother to tongue their load around to the side but leave it where it went in. Their frequent aspect—distended and blackened lower lip, jaw-wagging speech and a difficulty in shaping certain sounds, perhaps a trail of dried juice running down into stubble from one corner of the mouth—has been known upon sudden confrontation to set strong women screaming.

Women strong or weak accounted for a good part of the snuff consumed in Texas and elsewhere until not too long ago. But female dippers were dwindling in numbers even when I was young, and in the present degenerate days, when sexiness up to the age of seventy-five or so is an apparent common aim, the practice seems to be confined mainly to a few ancient and unreconstructedly country types. How sexy it may have been considered in its heyday I have no way of knowing, but some aging ladies whom I remember from long ago did manage to make it seem dainty, taking delicate quantities of the sovereign powder off of a little brush made from a twig of dogwood or peach or mesquite or some other fibrous, pleasantly flavored plant. Even using this method, though, others were not all that ladylike, and if we seek objective opinions we find that alien males have nearly always seen the habit as unattractive albeit somewhat monstrously fascinating, as witness the epistolary observations of a young Yankee soldier stationed in North Carolina in 1861, an ancestor of my wife's:

> There are a number of young girls about the Island some of whome are very good looking. But they spoil it all by indulging in the nasty habit of chewing snuff. . . . The modus operandi is as follows they get a piece of sweet brier wood, chew the end until it is after the style of a paint brush then dip in snuff and swab all over the mouth and lips, which gives them the appearance of a lot of dirty children who had been eating molasses candy so much for the style of Hatteras Belles. No danger of my getting spliced here.

Maybe, therefore, it is in part to snuff that we owe the renowned and oft-sung purity of Southern womanhood. . . .

Not long ago a rather petite and pretty blonde girl dressed in jeans and a flowered blouse came to our place in a pickup to inquire about buying some dairy goats. Though we had sold off all our Nubians some time before, interest in goats is a brotherhood and she and I talked for a while about different breeds and their quirks and qualities. From time to time as we spoke she turned her head aside and spat into the grass, so quietly and unobtrusively that I wouldn't have known what she was up to if I hadn't been a longtime student of such things. I didn't ask or comment, but I would have bet right there that she had derived the habit from a grandmother or great-grandmother of the old school, who knew well the rustic brown solace of snuff and had shared her knowledge down the generations. My heart swelled up within me. Tradition, praise the Lord, is not entirely dead.

Tobacco Without Smoke II: Chewers

While the mastication of tobacco has never to my knowledge been thought very socially suave—as, for instance, taking snuff by nose once was—in our part of the world it is only during the past forty years or so that it has come to be viewed with much opprobrium, at any rate among men. In my rather distant youth in Fort Worth—not exactly the fountainhead of national taste, but a fair-sized city even then, ruled by a relatively solid set of Southern-Western mores—courtrooms and other public places had plenty of gleaming brass cuspidors about for the benefit of chewers and so did a good many private offices and waiting rooms. For despite the reigning popularity of cigarettes and cigars, chewing held a long-established toehold in the masculine realms of the day, even at respectable levels.

Certain lawyers in particular whom I remember had fondness for the quid, as did some judges who rose from the legal ranks and occasionally sank back into them again when the pointing finger of electoral fortune swung elsewhere. But I knew doctors who partook also, though probably not in their offices, and oilmen who had picked up the habit on rigs where smoking was unwise, and a host of skilled jobholders of various sorts. Streetcar operators, for some reason, seemed to be chewers to a man and were furnished with a little brass trapdoor at their feet through which they spat between the tracks as their trolley sped and swayed along. By and large, storekeepers refrained at least while at their work, for they had to deal with customers of both sexes and one of the unwritten rules above a certain social line had always been that you didn't chew tobacco openly around ladies.

Most ladies for their part, whether urban or rural, were willing enough to let out of sight be out of mind and if they made any reference at all to the practice, it was with a moue of indulgent distaste. But some hated it consumingly, and woe was the chewer who married one of these unless he was a thirty-third-degree master of circumspection. A case in point was my maternal grandfather, a gentle agricultural immigrant to the Texas prairie from South Carolina, who like many of his generation was permanently a bit perplexed, I believe, by the lingering shock of the War and Reconstruction during which he had grown up. He had not a grain of circumspection in him or any other vices that I know of except a solid love for Brown's Mule plug tobacco, which was his bulwark. Beset on this account by not only a strong Baptist wife but two proper, married, city-dwelling daughters as well, when one or both of the daughters came on a weekend visit to back up his spouse's excoriations he would often seek refuge at his box-hive apiary below the house where none of these females cared to go, and though I was quite young when he died I can recall the good feel of sitting out there with him, enveloped in the hum of laboring German Black bees, as he nursed a friendly quid to calm his henpecked nerves and whittled profiled human figures for me out of slats of fruit-crate pine.

It is a great solacer, the chew, comparable in smoking to an aged and well-loved pipe. One old rancher I know, who uses no tobacco himself, recollects that in time of drouth or other trouble his bearded father would get up at one or two in the morning and go to the ranch house's dark living room to sit close by the dead fireplace chewing tobacco, sorting out his worries, spitting from time to time into the ashes, and by dawn ending up fairly cheerful. Such slow and ruminative use of nicotine has little in common with the fury of a tense cigarette smoker's puffing. It calms and gives perspective and is, to those of us who like it with or without our ladies' acquiescence (approval being too much to ask, we know), one of nature's true boons.

It is pleasant to be able to report that this noble practice seems to have had a mild renaissance in the past few years—that is to say among middleclass sorts, for with laborers and countrymen it never lost its vogue. If, as the old cigar ad said, spit is a horrid word, our Surgeon General's intimation that cigarette may be a worse one has set reflective or spooked smokers to thinking in other directions. The pipe and the cigar were given much higher marks than the cigarette by the said SG's statistics and many have changed over to them. But the fact is that those statistics were derived from lifelong devotees of pipes and cigars, who seldom inhale smoke, whereas cigarette smokers who switch nearly always do, so that they're

probably getting more "tar" and other abominations in their lungs now than they did from the filtered cigarettes they gave up. Logic might suggest flat abandonment of the weed, but logic is a bit mathematical for many of us nicotine heads, and so we explore the other avenues that tradition offers. Though snuff has its points, the nasal mode of taking it is a bit alien and queer, and the old Southern way of folding it into the lip has very unfortunate connotations roundabout, as we have seen, based on equally unfortunate reality. This leaves the quid, whose connotations in truth are not all that glorious either among moderns, but which can be unobtrusive if used prudently and does possess for us older conservative types the virtue of having once been acceptable in fairly polite male circles, even if it does require a little spitting to get rid of excess juice.

In female circles I have a hard time believing it will ever have much appeal, either as something to do or as a spectator sport, though of course I may be hidebound in this view. In topsy-turvy times nearly anything can happen, and conceivably the sexist monopoly heretofore enjoyed by men in the realm of chewing tobacco may sooner or later tempt some feminists into joining us as we munch. If so, they might consider adopting as a patron saint that historic Parker County lady, a Mrs. Rippy, who once faced down some raiding Comanches (male) by fishing a plug from between her un-brassiered breasts and biting off a hunk while she cursed and glared at them. . . .

Chewing tobacco comes in three main forms these days, the best known of which is the kind Mrs. Rippy used, a dark compressed brick enclosed in a wrapper of light-brown leaf. Nearly all of the numerous brands of plug, each with its hooked supporters, are impregnated to some degree with molasses for flavor and cohesiveness. In the so-called "natural leaf" sorts this admixture is rather light, but in a good many of the others it is heavy enough to give the tobacco a sticky texture and a candy sweetness in the mouth, and some of the other attributes of candy too. A dentist with a rural and small-town practice once told me he could spot many chewers easily—not by stains, for contrary to slanderous rumor chewing sullies teeth less than smoking does if the chewer brushes daily, but by where their cavities occurred. A real quid man with a taste for sweet tobacco would have most of his caries in a clump on the outside of his lower molars, righthand or left according to where he usually kept his sugared chew.

Plug tobacco is compact and easily hidden on the person, and since it expands somewhat in the mouth a small bit can give fair satisfaction without a great deal of mulling about and consequent spitting. Therefore it's rather well suited to the purposes of sub-rosa indoor users, who are denied access to cuspidors these days and have to search about for potted plants or men's rooms if their chew gets unruly in its production of strong fluids. (One lawyer friend of mine uses wastebaskets when he can't find anything else, but on the other hand he's not a very sub-rosa type either.) To use plug, though, you ought to like it, and some people find this hard. I've heard that when the habit had more standing a few premium brands of superb flavor were available at high prices, some of them made from the true Havana leaf, but these are different times and many kinds now have a "pluggy" edge of rancidity in their taste that not all chewers admire.

A seldom-seen variation on the plug is the old-fashioned twist, usually made by growers out of their own leaf by forming it when damp into a tight-spiraled rope which is then doubled back and retwisted on itself. Twist can be unbelievably strong; some that I ordered in quantity from Tennessee a couple of years ago, fire-cured stuff, turned out to be so imperious that I ended up feeding it bit by bit to my goats, who thought it gourmet fare. I need to add that this wasn't sadism on my part, for not only do goats like tobacco but it also does them good; in the days before modern veterinary antihelminthics made an appearance it was the drug of choice for worming them. Human chewers have a general heartening belief, probably valid, that the habit will keep *them* from getting worms, though a small still voice wonders how much of an advantage this is in a society that has largely vanquished such parasites.

A second main form of chew is what used to be known as "scrap," a homely term that has likely been euphemized into something else by now, though if so I haven't heard what. Consisting of coarse, usually syruped shreds, it comes packed in foil-lined pouches, and on grocery store shelves the main brands—Beech Nut, Red Man, Mail Pouch, etc.—are a familiar sight. So elsewhere are the hugely lumped cheek and hearty expectoration characteristic of most of its users. It is strangely hard to take a little-bitty wad of scrap and just tuck it away for nursing. A large dangling three-finger pinch is the rule, and after you've draped it into your mouth you have to more or less bale it with your tongue and side teeth; in the parlance of chewers it "works you to death," demanding to be rolled about and gnawed. In consequence those who favor it tend to be either outdoor workers or types who are proud of their habit's masculinity and like to exhibit it—baseball players, rodeo cowboys, and such, along with fans who admire them.

Another rodeo cowboy and athlete, however, the amiable Walt Garrison—at least he seems amiable enough in the TV commercials—has lately been hitting a hard promotional lick for a very popular third form of oral tobacco that is the least showy of all, or can be. This is the granulated wet kind sold in flat cylindrical waxed boxes with tin lids, known in the Midwest and to some extent down here as "snoose"—from, I understand, the Danish-Swedish *snus* for snuff, which indicates its ultimate geographic origin and has bearing on a controversy concerning what the substance really is. The United States Tobacco Company, which manufactures all the brands of it I've seen (and which must be cleaning up), has muddied the question rather thoroughly. Its original stout, sweetish-salty version called Copenhagen is labeled forth-rightly "snuff" on the box, but of three subsequent products flavored with wintergreen, mint, and (no comment) rasp-berry, one is described as "chewing tobacco" and the other two as "smokeless tobacco."

Such skilled semantic footwork almost certainly has to do with snuff's American reputation, which as we have noted before is especially poor in urban reaches of the once snuff-happy Southland. The same reputation, though, appears to be why certain users maintain hotly that snoose *is* snuff. Some of its burgeoning popularity, undoubtedly in part because of Walt Garrison's rugged grin, has been among youths of goat-roping and/or footballing propensities, who carry it in jeans hip pockets where the container's round shape is unmistakable, or sometimes even flaunt it in special pouches hanging from their belts. Though many of them, maybe most, come from the urban or small-town middle classes, the image they yearn to project is anything but bourgeois, and having descried that in bourgeois eyes snuff is very nasty, they're vehement in insisting that what they use is snuff and what they do is dip it. Occasional bumper stickers on pickup trucks underline the point. In fairness, I haven't heard our amiable and prosperous friend Walt put things in this way; he calls the stuff merely tobacco, and wintergreen Skoal is his flavor.

The trouble is that anyone who has put in time around real dippers knows that the only material that deserves to be called snuff is the true, the blissful, the sometimes consum-mately repulsive brown powder of our Southern heritage. In these terms, the kids' pretensions are rather pathetic. For pure horribleness, they couldn't start to compete with even a medium-nasty front-lipper of Levi Garrett or Rooster, try as hard as they might, for their ammunition is just not up to the job. It compacts readily into a manageable wad, settles well for long nursing, and doesn't keep sending its effluvium all over the mouth to encourage wild dark salivation. In short, it may be a hybrid form, but it acts very comfortably like chewing tobacco.

Snoose sneaked in on Texas at some point, not being traditional here. As a long-hallowed institution up North, it must have entered this region before the Second World War, when I first saw it in use among Midwestern farm boys in the service, but if so it hadn't made enough of a dent in the market to become well known. During one period or another it gained acceptance in the oil patch and lately it has been gaining the same thing widely elsewhere, for the reasons given above and other related ones that are clear enough. A little of it goes a long way, both in kick and in time, and unless you take on too much you seldom have to offend anyone's sensibilities by spitting after it's well established in your cheek. It makes the best secret chew available, and that is what a surprisingly varied lot of men are looking for just now.

Two or three years ago I was talking with a banker at his vice-presidential desk. He is an urbane sort but has been around, having begun his working life as an oilfield roustabout in the North Texas Red Rolling Plains. We had arrived at an ever-absorbing subject, the pains of stopping smoking, when he hesitated, grinned broadly, reached into the side pocket of his tailored sharkskin coat, and briefly flashed a round box of Copenhagen.

"The hell with cigarettes," he said. "This is all I need. I'm right back where I started out."

· · ·

Being inclined to read up on whatever subject it is that grabs me at the moment, I've trodden some weed-grown literary byways in my time, and once in a witty and unsubstantial eighteenth-century book I ran across a classification of nasal snuffers according to their manner of handling the treasured dust. Described therein were the Pinch Supercilious, the Pinch Ecclesiastical, the Pinch Haughty and its counterpart the Pinch Self-effacing, and so forth. In like mode, I suppose, one could examine chewers. We've already glanced at the two extremes—the Chew Surreptitious, a tiny quid nursed in secret for hours through conferences with clients and board meetings and even cocktail parties, and the Chew Ostentatious, that large juicy lump affected by pitchers and bronc-riders and others who perform for the public in the open air. In between these are the other kinds, including such oddments as the Chew Cinematic, seen in real life only among callow beginners. Its manipulator, most often either a stubbled villain or a crusty picturesque in Westerns, works his jaw up and down in exaggerated wagging rhythm and spits noisily every fifteen seconds, thus using up, one would be willing to bet, enough tobacco to require the services of an extra pack horse on trips.

But most common among us ordinary folks is the Chew Philosophical, a moderate wad of the type and flavor of tobacco preferred by the philosopher in question, who after working it into the proper shape and consistency tucks it away against his jaw and holds it thereafter with quiet pleasure and only occasional expulsion of fluid, stealthy or otherwise as conditions demand. For circumstances have much to do with one's manner of chewing. A usual practitioner of the surreptitious or the philosophical style may, when outdoors by himself or in tolerant company, indulge himself in the Chew Generous, aiming frequent jets of brown juice at stones and spiders and cow patties and the entrance holes of red-ant beds and enjoying the process hugely.

Once I knew a Generous Chewer who most enjoyed aiming at people, or seemed to. He was part-owner and scale man at a cotton compress where I had a twenty-cent-an-hour summer job at sixteen or so, rolling heavy bales around warehouses and docks with a two-wheeled hand truck in the company of large black men and a few other kids like myself. When we stood in line at the hanging-beam scales to have our bales lifted and weighed, we had to keep a sharp wary eye on this gentleman—call him Lonnie Vaughan. He always had a jowlful of scrap tobacco and had the habit of spitting often and abruptly in almost any direction, swiveling his small, sandy, snakelike, unsmiling head to left or right or even straight around to his rear, then without a pause loosing a copious squirt. It put me in a state of nerves, for that was not long after *Reader's Digest* had printed its first daring article on the horrors of syphilis, from which Mister Lonnie was said to suffer, and I was dead certain that if a single drop of that juice hit my skin I'd catch it. Jobs were scarce in those Depression days, though, and I don't remember hearing anyone complain.

If all this delight came without internal hazards and difficulties there would be a lot more chewers around than there are, regardless of protests from women and other non-users who think the habit unesthetic. The main effect of chewing— call it narcotic or toxic or whatever you like—derives from absorption of nicotine through the mouth's mucous tissues, there being no jolt or high like that of inhaled smoke but rather a steady and low-keyed sense of all's being right with the world, more or less. Obviously, however, not all the fluid generated by a quid is expectorated by the user even if he tends toward the Chew Cinematic. Some, along with the alkaloids it carries, goes inexorably to the stomach and some stomachs, I have to report, don't like this at all.

The problem is not at all new. American aborigines had been happily consuming tobacco in all its forms for ages before whites arrived and seized upon the weed for their own delectation, and many of them who chewed it had the habit of mixing it beforehand with a powder made from lime or burned shells, just as is done with coca leaf and betel nut. These Indians' modern equivalent is the fellow who carries some antacid tablets in his shirt pocket and downs one whenever his chew seems to be catching up with him, but even this doesn't always work. Some people are simply not made for the quid.

One such that I heard about lately was a young doctor in a Texas coastal city, who had developed a hero fix on a senior member of the group of surgeons with whom he worked and sought to imitate him in every way possible, right down to his distinctive methods of tying sutures, wearing a hat, knuckling an ear, and inquiring benevolently as to postoperative patients' bowel habits. The older man, a rugged former athlete, was fond of golf and while on the links always munched a large wad of Tinsley Red Tag plug. His disciple played with him and after some hesitation took up the other habit too, and with the aid of Maalox got away with it for two or three rounds. But then one day he tensed up over a close putt, swallowed the wrong way, and barfed all over the fourteenth green in front of his hero and two other golfers, who nearly fell down laughing. At last report he had gone back to Vantages and was thinking seriously of switching from surgery to pediatrics.

Hence our society is probably not in much danger of being taken over by tobacco chewers, and this is very likely a good thing. But I suspect that as long as there are men who spend

time regularly outdoors there will be chewers, and that some
of these will carry chewing back indoors with them, though
generally in secretive fashion. For the practice is not an old
one without reason, and the reason has little to do with show-
off masculinity or juvenile would-be nastiness. It has to do
with quiet pleasure and equanimity. Nobody but an ironhead
can maintain, in the light of present medical knowledge, that
tobacco in this or any other form is good for the human body.
But the body, as all but mechanists know, is only part of a
man, and chewers believe whether rightly or wrongly that
they have a hold on one thing that is good for another part.

One's Own Sole Ground

Possibly because of the more or less steady, change-fostered bewilderment that is our modern lot, a good many of us have developed the habit of jamming one another—and sometimes, for that matter, ourselves—into convenient categories like Young Executive, Welfare Black, Gay, Middleclass Housewife, Hardhat, Hippie, Educated Brown, Gun Nut, Used-car Salesman, etc. The media and the PR industry assist this trend with a zeal born of their veneration for all usable clichés and lumpings, and the categories have the further advantage of being stackable, as in Gay Hardhatted Gun Nut. In regard to us country-dwellers, city types often cherish a classification called Hick, Redneck, Sturdy Peasant, or something on that

order which makes them feel more easy of mind when they
stray beyond the developments and the junk yards and see
actual human beings out here in the fields and pastures and
seated beneath the overhangs of crossroads filling stations.

It won't really work, of course, any more than most of the
other categories will, stackable or not, for on closer scrutiny
the Sturdy Peasants—like, say, Middleclass Housewives—
subdivide into so many disorderly groupings that the would-be
categorizer is swiftly again dunked in bewilderment. However, one broad class of country people may be worth eyeing
separately, at any rate for certain purposes. Its members can
be pleasant or grouchy, slow or bright, young or old, short
or tall or poor or rich, possessed of thousands of spreading
acres or modest homestead tracts. But they're all possessed of
something in the way of rural real estate. They are Landowners, a fact which bestows on most of them at least one
shared conviction, or illusion: they believe they not only own
but actually govern whatever patch of the earth's crusty surface to which title has been vouchsafed them by inheritance,
gift, or purchase. They are at one with W. S. Blunt's Old
Squire, who thought he was his own sole king upon his own
sole ground.

This sovereignty is a mite imperiled these days, or at least
many of its holders think it is. The shift of political potency
to urban areas, begun with the reapportionment of legislative
and congressional districts years ago and reflecting a tremendous demographic change, is now resulting in a rash of
countryward-aimed regulations and laws that presume to tell
landowners quite a bit more than they're used to hearing about
what they can or can't do on their land. Most being ecological
or humanitarian in drift, intended to abate pollution, preserve
wildlife, better the lot of migrant workers, and so on, the
rural antagonism they arouse is directed not only at the government entities that seek to enforce them—EPA, OSHA,

ESSA, et al.—but at the city-bred environmentalists and liberals whose inclinations they express. The stud-buzzard bugaboo of all, still only a threatening rumor in most places, is land-use regulation, whereby the countryside would be zoned, in effect, and proper employment of its parts prescribed by urban fiat.

Embattled, or seeing themselves so, the Sturdy Peasants close ranks and espouse tight positions that some of them might not have cared for just a few years since. I used to know, for instance, quite a few intelligent, born-and-bred countrymen who could see as clearly as any Sierra Clubber the dangerous wrongfulness of such wholesale poisons as the chlorinated-hydrocarbon insecticides and varmint-killing 1080, but since federal restrictions have been put on their use these free spirits seem either to have shut up or to have joined the rural chorus singing harmoniously of deprivation. The trend shows up in an admirable ranching newspaper to which I subscribe, published in San Angelo, which not only gives a good picture of the state of the world as it affects cattle, sheep, and goat husbandry week by week, but also prints a fair amount of fine, dry, tough, West Texas humor and some excellent stuff on range management and sidelights of Southwestern history. And sprinkled through its pages also, you find news items and sometimes longish, well-researched articles relating to one phase or another of the government's determination to foul up ranchers' established ways of doing things, whether in terms of predator control, a ban on the use of 2,4,5-T, the curtailment of grazing leases on public lands in New Mexico, or whatever. Replete with examples of often quite real bureaucratic ineptitude and critical, by implication or otherwise, of the urban electorate that establishes bureaucrats' functions and urges them on in their lunacy, these articles accurately mirror the angers and apprehensions of the paper's readership.

It's hard to say how much of this is really new. Slightly paranoid antipathy toward outsiders, especially city outsiders, has never been far below the surface in us rustics since mud-brick civilization began, and whether it's getting worse nowadays is moot. One way or the other, it amounts to little in comparison with other tensions that currently rack all people, between sexes, races, generations, regions, nations. But it can be both fascinating and a bit worrisome if you stand close to it and are a sort of hybrid city-rustic yourself. Living on the land most of the time, I notice it mainly in the changing (or is it?) feeling of countrymen, including that part of myself, toward the outsiders we actually see in our own precincts, the hunters and fishermen and geologizers and similar wanderers who favor us intermittently with their presence. Some few landowners are still quite easygoing, tolerating everything from strayed bulls and uninvited hunters to brush trysters and arrowhead seekers as mere facts of life, not worth roiling one's stomach acids about unless they do notable damage to pastures, crops, or livestock. Others, of my ilk, would like to be that benign but have been forced by experience into wariness, particularly of strangers with weapons. And still others bring to the exercise of ownership the forthright territoriality of red hornets and Doberman pinschers, resenting and resisting all trespass.

Here in Texas many old-line ranchers have long been thus hotly jealous of their frontiers, which seems a bit strange in view of the open-range origins of their trade but may well trace back to the bitter fence-war era of the 1880's, when barbed wire brought the concept of private land ownership quite abruptly to our ancestral prairies and anyone who wanted to hold on to his slice of them had better wax fiercely possessive. Within my lifetime, in days of cheaper help and fewer effete scruples, the boundary fences of certain large ranches were still patrolled by armed mounted men under orders, it was said and widely believed, to ventilate intruders on sight; and dramatic, whether true or not, were the tales about persons who had crawled through those fences and never been seen again. Of late such princeliness has grown more costly and has been perhaps further weakened by a thinning of fiber in the old princes' inheritors. But the gist of the attitude lingers down, and to this day in most ranching sections not many savvy roamers will cross even three rusty strands of wire drooping between rotten posts without knowing who holds the other side in fee simple, and how he'll react to their presence if he sees them.

Having grown up around such ways, I remember being surprised in Old World places by the apparent freedom with which villagers and landless countrymen, or even city vacationers, ranged through the holdings of their patrician compatriots—picnicking, gathering deadwood fuel and wild fruits and nuts and herbs and fungi, and otherwise disporting themselves. A closer look generally revealed some fairly ferocious rules relating to the sacrosanctity of game, fish, crops, and a few other things, given force by what was left of a class structure and the customs of a thousand years or more. Even so, it was impressive, and except among a few rule-resistant gypsies and poachers, it worked.

Vestiges of that sort of tolerance remain in some of our own older farming regions, where live most of the easygoing landowners I've mentioned. But these are areas, like much of Europe, where people have had several or many generations to learn to stay off one another's nerves through observance of unwritten rules, and it takes only a few outsiders ignorant of the rules to blow the whole pattern to pieces. And since outsiders proliferate practically everywhere in these times of mobility that is sometimes upward but more often sidewise, the isles of rural tolerance tend to shrink and vanish. When I was young and used to go quail shooting with my father and

uncles in a long-settled part of South Texas, you could stop
at almost any farm or small ranch to ask about hunting there,
and if you had minimally passable manners and had recently
bathed and shaved you were as often as not welcomed and
told sure, go ahead. Now I fear you'd meet with little but curt
or at best matter-of-fact rebuff, maybe softened a mite by the
information that the place's hunting has been leased. This
leasing, unknown a few decades back except in deer sections
but widespread now, does bring landowners some extra cash
each year, but the main reason most of them like it is that it
limits interlopers to a few known individuals and reestab-
lishes a set of rules and customs.

Unknown individuals are the losers, at least those of them
with an urge to percolate about the landscape, and they have
a harder time in Texas than in those other Western states with
vast reaches of public land for recreational use by one and all.
Nimrods suffer most, for Sturdy Peasants have convenient
stereotypic classifications also, and for most of them the City
Hunter is a disquieting figure. There is reason for this feeling.
I've been a hunter all my life and will likely remain one for
as much of the rest of it as physical condition permits, and I
have a good many hunters for friends, most of them mild and
skillful men with a knowledge of country ways. But I find
that it takes a major effort these days to identify with the
hunting clan at large, being a landowner myself and remem-
bering three or four of my beasts that have been perforated
over the years by accident or intention, as well as having
listened over and over to fellow countrymen's recountals of
tromped-down fences, gates disastrously left open, grain and
hay crops squashed and rutted by ATV's, tin barns or cisterns
or windmills riddled with holes, seven-millimeter magnum
slugs whining by someone's spouse's left ear as she hangs out
the wash, and so on.

Years ago I knew slightly a venerable rancher far to the

west who, with the sole help of his spare wife, ran cattle on a swatch of remote rough foothills and low mountains where pronghorns and mule deer ranged. He was cranky but sociable enough, as people in thinly inhabited regions incline toward being, and had seldom minded having hunters on his land if he knew them or liked their looks. But one morning early a pair of beefy unknowns came down his entrance road in a new Continental, parked it outside his yard fence where the road turned to a rocky jeep trail, took out rifles and lunch bags, and aimed themselves for the hills without a glance at the house.

He came out. "Where you fellows headed?" he asked.

They stopped and looked around. "Going hunting," the bigger one said.

"Maybe you are and maybe you ain't."

"The hell we ain't, old-timer," said the big one, and levered a cartridge into the chamber of his gun, though without pointing it in any particular direction.

"I see," said the rancher stroking his jaw. "Well, I guess you will if you want to, because I ain't very big on killing or getting killed. But I'll tell you one thing."

"Like what?"

"Like I got pretty near a case of thirty-thirty shells in the bedroom, and not a damn thing to do but just sit here on the front steps all day and shoot holes in that car. I bet I can even bust the engine block if I keep on hitting one place."

They studied him and mumbled a bit between themselves, then got back into the big sedan and drove off, leaving behind some new City Hunter material for local lore to digest. By the time I knew him the old man had quit letting anybody hunt on the ranch, even friends. So had most of his neighbors.

But hunters, while they're a prime source of rural qualms, are only one form of alien invader, and your truly obsessed landowner gets just about as upset over some other forms as well. The visitations of male adolescents, for example, are seldom regarded with joy even when they leave the customary twenty-two at home. Running usually in small packs, charged with directionless energy, given horrid mobility by the internal-combustion engine, they egg one another on in senselessness and when confronted with an isolated homestead whose owners are away can on occasion create a degree of chaos that Attila's lads would not at all mind claiming. (Yes, I know about all the good kids around, but I'm retailing a body of legend with, unfortunately, some roots in fact. . . .) Sometimes their spoor can be rather interesting. At the country place outside of Fort Worth where we used to live, such a troop came around one day in our absence, let the locked house alone except for hurling rocks through a couple of windows and splintering some porch furniture, but at the barn dumped out the contents of every box and crate they could find. They left most of the stuff strewn where it fell but lugged fourteen musty volumes of Sir Walter Scott's prose works fifty yards away to throw them into a stock trough, whose float they thoughtfully broke off so that the valve was still spouting water when we got back two days later. With plenty of other books around the barn, I wondered why the Master of Abbotsford had been thus favored, and conjured up the image of a frail, stern, hated, spinster highschool teacher musing out the last stages of the Gothic Southern dream, trying to ram *Ivanhoe* and *The Bride of Lammermoor* into barbaric hotrod brains, and evoking this slantwise revenge. I didn't wonder why *we* had been thus favored: it was because, like the mountain, we were there.

So it is that many of us benevolent lordlings who would like to be tolerant in the Old World manner grow less hospitable year by year, while others who were always inclined toward tight awareness of their dominion become little short of rabid. Probably the feistiest specimens are those with land bordered by parks, reservoirs, highways, and other accessible havens from which incursions can and do proceed, and a current emphasis on public outdoor recreation is dimly viewed among them. One fellow I know of, who has parlayed a hilly, rather small holding into a species of gold mine by crisscrossing it with dirt-bike trails and charging city cyclists five dollars a head to play there on weekends, is hardly spoken to by his deafened neighbors any more. Jeffersonian in their essence, they have come to agree in at least one respect with their patron figure's arch antithesis A. Hamilton: "Your public, sir, is a great beast."

A battleground that has shaped up in recent years lies along the Texas rivers. State-owned streams which twenty years ago were little frequented by anyone but people living beside them and a few local anglers, they have now become pleasure routes, at least when they're flowing and the mosquitoes aren't too bad, for numerous canoes and kayaks and rubber rafts. The enthusiasts who paddle these craft are mainly nature-minded and innocuous, but they are anathema to riverbank landowners with a lifetime behind them of regarding those abutting waters as their own and not having to fret about fires and racket and litter in the bottomlands. The conflict is often unpleasant but occasionally somewhat funny, as when an ardent canoeist of my acquaintance, a conservative and in fact fairly testy landowner himself though city-based, was menaced in his camp on the Frio one morning by an enraged lady goat rancher with a gun. "I wasn't even inside her fence, but I told her I had a ranch too and understood how she felt," my friend reported, disgruntled and aggrieved. "But the crazy old biddy kept on waving that Model Ninety-four and hollering she didn't care what I understood, just get the hell out of there."

It would be nice to end this discussion on a hopeful note, envisioning some sort of rapprochement between the rednecked son of the soil and his white-naped urban counterpart, wherein each would share out the best of what his own world has to offer. Certainly the homogenizing influence of things like TV and the readiness with which countrymen flow cityward and urbanites, when able, toward the land these days should militate in favor of better relations. In pretty terrain within a couple of hours' driving distance of large cities much acreage is owned absentee by townsfolk who visit it on weekends and later settle there in retirement, and a major fact of this century of change, seen sometimes as tragic, has been the enormous migration of country people to metropolises. With such mixing, it would seem the rough edges ought to wear off of old enmities and suspicions.

In some ways I guess they do, but there are complications. For one thing, assimilation at the other end of the migratory route isn't always what the migrants have in mind. City landowners often remain city people in manners and attitudes and most of all in the opinion of neighboring rurals, and the lonesome-misfit plight of erstwhile farmers and their womenfolk on the streets of Dee-troit City and other magnetic urbs is a poignant major theme of country music. Another trouble is that many of those who do manage to shoulder their way through to acceptance in their new surroundings tend to take on protective coloration and to look back at what they came from in distaste; country women transplanted to careerdom or suburbia, for instance, have a frequent scorn of rural ways, and some of the most violently possessive, snuff-dippingly rustic landowners I've known had done their growing up in town and had made the money there with which to buy their farms or ranches. And if, as I seem to discern, the pitch of paranoia has been rising a note or two out here on the hills and prairies, it appears to be matched by a touch of the same shrill ailment among metropolitans in relation to us peasants, as demonstrated not only by laws and regulations that chew

on what countrymen see as their rights but also, more pain-
fully perhaps, by the great urban success of bucolic scare-
figures like the murderous yokels of *Easy Rider* and *Deliver-
ance*'s buggerly backwoodsmen.

Maybe this is our hopeful note: that human difference and
variousness do hang on in spite of all. Obviously, at any rate,
everything can't be wrong in a world where such honorably
ancient dislikes and mistrusts retain their traditional force.

A Loser

It was the kind of farm auction that mainly countrymen and a few implement dealers attend, for it was in an out-of-the-way part of the upper West Cross Timbers and the classified ad announcing it in the Fort Worth paper had mentioned no churns, crocks, wagonwheels, or other aging curiosities of the sort that lure crowds of city people to such affairs. There was to be a disposal of everything on hand, including the farm itself—"125 a. sandy land, 45 in cultivation, rest improved grass and timber, 2 tanks, barn, new brick home 3 b.r. 2 baths, all furnishings." Though it lay about two hours north of my own place and I'm not much addicted to those sellout auctions—melancholy events nearly always, aromatic with defeat and often with death—I drove up that Saturday in late winter because among the items listed for sale was an Allis-Chalmers grain combine of the antiquated type that is pulled and powered by a tractor.

In my rough area these relatively small harvesting machines, none of them less than about twenty years old, are still in demand if they've been kept in working order. Most of our field land is in little tracts strewn about between the hills, and even when you can find a custom combine operator willing to bring his shiny self-propelled behemoth to your place for the sake of reaping just twelve or twenty or thirty acres of oats or wheat, he will most likely balk when he gets a good look at the narrow rocky lanes and steep stream crossings through which it must be jimmied to arrive at its work. As a result we often let our cattle keep on grazing winter grain fields past mid-March, when they ought to be taken off if harvest is intended, or we cut and bale the stuff green for hay. But sometimes when you'd like a bin full of grain to carry your horses and goats through winter and maybe to fatten a steer or so for slaughter, you wish you had a bit more of the sort of control that possession of your own varied if battered machinery gives.

A front had pushed heavy rains through the region the day before and the morning was bleak, with gray solid mist scudding not far overhead and the northwest wind jabbing the pickup toward the shoulder as I drove. It grew bleaker after I left our limestone hills, with their liveoaks and cedars that stay green all year, and came into country where only a few brown leaves still fluttered on winter-bare post oaks and briers and hardwood scrub. Sandy fields lay reddish and wet and sullen under the norther's blast, and in some rolling pastures, once tilled but now given over to grass and brush, gullies had chewed through the sand and eaten deep into the russet clay underneath. Outlying patches of such soil and vegetation oc-

cur even in my own county, and for that matter since childhood I've known and visited this main Cross Timbers belt, a
great finger-shape of sand and once-stately oak woods poking
down into Texas from the Red River. But it has always had
a queerly alien feel for me, in part undoubtedly because I
grew up surrounded by limestone and black prairie dirt and
the plants they favor and, with the parochialism dear to the
human heart, I simply like them.

Others for their part prefer the sand, and locals of this
stamp seemed to make up a majority of the hundred and fifty
or so people who were standing around in clumps when I
parked alongside a narrow dirt road, slithered up a clay hill
past a low suburban-style house, and entered the farmyard
where, arranged in a wide ellipse, stood the relics and trophies
of someone's ruptured love affair with the soil. Bushel baskets
and nail kegs filled with random hand tools and pipe fittings
and bolts and log chains and mason jars and whatnot. A section harrow, three tandem disks, plows of various sorts, a
row planter, a cultivator, a grain drill, a hay swather, two
balers of which one was riddled with rust and good only for
parts cannibalization, a corral holding twenty or more good
crossbred beef cows with their calves, a tin barn half full of
baled Coastal Bermuda and, as the ad had promised, other
items too numerous to mention, though I can't help mention-
ing one: a large and gleaming tuba. Much of the farm machinery had a scarred third-hand look quite familiar to me, for
it was the kind of stuff that we marginal small-timers tend to
end up with. But this fellow had invested in a much greater
variety of it than I had ever ventured to, and here and there
sat something fairly expensive with the sheen of relative new-
ness on it—a good medium-sized tractor, a heavy offset-disk
plow, a fancy wheeled dirt scoop with hydraulic controls. . . .

The blocky orange shape of the A.-C. combine loomed at
the far end of the ellipse, and as I walked toward it wind-

hunched locals in caps and heavy jackets and muddy boots viewed me with taciturn distaste, another outlander plunked down among them to run the bidding up and make them shell out more for whatever it was they had their eyes and hearts set on. Two of them were studying the combine and stopped talking when I came near, but started again in lower tones after I began jiggling levers and checking belts and chains and opening flaps to peer at intricacies inside the big box. Its paint job wasn't bad, so it had been kept under cover for at least some of its long life, and those metal working parts that came in contact with moving grain and straw and chaff were shiny-bright in testimony, I thought, of fairly recent use, a hawk-eyed Holmesian observation confirmed by one of the other interested parties.

"They cut twenty-four acres with it last summer," he said to his friend. "I know because I seen it. It didn't blow hardly no oats out on the ground."

"What about the canvases?" I asked, for those wide ribbed belts that elevate materials from the cutter bar to the machine's complicated interior matter greatly, and are expensive to replace if worn out or rotten from neglect.

He snapped his stubbled jaw shut and glared but had to answer, minimally. "In the barn," he said.

I found them on a shelf there and they looked all right too. The combine was worth trying to buy, though while examining it I had begun to have misgivings about towing its eleven-and-a-half-foot width over the fifteen miles of narrow muddy humpbacked roads, with waterfilled ditches, that I had traversed since leaving pavement, and then maneuvering it through the Saturday traffic of three fair-sized county seats that stood between this place and home. However, these thoughts were cut short by the crackle and burp of a bullhorn near the house and a jovial brassy voice announcing the auction's start. Together with most of the others I moved toward

the scarlet pickup from whose bed the bullhorn blared, but a few dogged figures remained beside implements or other objects they had chosen, establishing what they hoped was priority and waiting for the sale to come to them.

The auctioneer was a pro as nearly all are these days, stetsoned and paunched and lump-jawed with sweet Red Fox tobacco. He knew a few of the people present—Western-clad and cliquish, probably dealers—and jollied them by name between spells of ribba-dibba chanting and exhortation to higher bids as an assistant held up the containers of smaller stuff to view and they were sold off batch by batch. Loading the cold moving air with urgent sound, his amplified voice fanned greed and fuzzed rational thought among less inured listeners, as it was intended to do, but the crowd wasn't a prosperous one and at this early stage the bidding stayed low. I felt a twinge of avarice as a basket of good wrenches and pliers and screwdrivers and such, worth probably eighty or ninety dollars at retail, went for $4.75, but forced myself into the reflection that I already owned at least one specimen of every tool there—as, probably, did the grim skinny oldster who bought them and bore them away in triumph. . . . The pickup inched forward along the line of ranked items as they were sold, and when it reached the farming implements the visiting dealers moved in for the kill and things began to get hotter, to the disgruntlement of us amateurs. Thwarted, a young farmer delivered a hard sodden kick to the beam of the handsome yellow offset-disk over which I had earlier seen him practically salivating, but for whose sake he had been unwilling or unable to top the seven hundred and fifty dollars it brought, about half of its market value even second-hand. "Them son of a bitches sure make things hard," he said.

I was looking at a hatless thin-clad man who sat on the edge of the pickup's bed beside the auctioneer. He was in his forties, pale and slight and balding and with the pinched waxy look of sickness on him, maybe even of cancer, and as I watched his dark worrier's eyes switch anxiously from bidder to bidder and saw the down-tug of his lips when something sold far too low, I knew very well who he was. He was the erstwhile lord of this expanse of wet sand and red mud, the buyer and mender and operator of a good bit too much machinery for forty-five arable acres, the painstaking nurturer and coddler of those fat penned cows, the player perhaps of a tuba, the builder of a hip-roofed brick-veneer castle, 3 b.r. 2 baths, from which to defend his woman and his young against the spears of impending chaos. Except that chaos, as is its evil custom, had somehow stolen in on him unawares and confounded all his plans. He was, in short, the Loser.

"I got a scoop," the auctioneer cried. "I got a big red dirt scoop. I got a great big pretty red dirt scoop that'll dig you a ditch and build you a terrace and haul one whole cubic yard of gravel or sand up out of your creek bed, and all you got to do is touch a little lever and she dumps it right where you want it. Eight-ply tires and the whole thing just about new from the looks of it. What you say, men?"

"Thirty-five," ventured one of his auditors in a tentative voice. I saw the Loser twitch and tense, and surmised that to him, for whatever reason, the scoop had special meaning, as occasional implements do.

"That ain't no bid, it's an insult," said the auctioneer.

"Cylinder's busted," the bidder answered with a defensive air, and I remembered noting that the arm of a hydraulic piston on the scoop was bent and useless, though repair or replacement probably wouldn't cost much.

"Urba durba dibba rubba hurty-fie," said the auctioneer in abandonment of the subject. "Hurty-fie hurty-fie hurty-fie, who say fitty? Fitty, fitty, fitty, fitty, durba dubba ibba dibby who say forty-fie? Forty-fie, forty-fie, come on, folks. . . ."

"Forty!" somebody yelled.

A Loser

The Loser rose trembling to his full five foot seven or so beside the large auctioneer, and his unamplified voice was reedy
but the feeling behind it carried it out over the crowd. "God-
amighty, boys," he said. "I paid out three seventy-five for that
thing not six months ago and the fellow I got it from he hadn't
never used it but twice. Another fellow come by one day when
I was digging a tank with it and he wanted to give me five
hundred. That there's a *good* machine. I just can't see . . ."
And sat down, staring at his toes. As if in imitation, many
in the crowd looked earthward toward their own muddy
footwear, and an almost visible feeling enveloped us like thick
gas, and was not blown away by the steady wind. Faced with
erosion of the mood he had been building, the auctioneer spat
brown juice and stared briefly, cynically, toward the gray
horizon before returning to the fray. "Man's right," he said.
"Listen to him, boys. It's a good scoop. You got to remember what the Bible says, Thou shalt not steal."
Urba dibby, etc., and in the end the scoop fetched ninety
bucks, which may have been a bit more than it would have
brought without the little man's outburst. Nobody, it seemed,
really wanted a scoop, and the dealers for their own private
reasons were not interested. The Loser shortly thereafter got
down from the pickup and went to what was at that point still
his house, followed by numerous furtive eyes.
"Poor booger," somebody said.
In large part our lingering fog of feeling was made up of
shame, of the guilt most of us had brought along with us to
the sale, knowing that if we found any bargains there it would
be because of someone else's tough luck. Some of us hadn't
been aware that we carried this load until we heard the Loser
speak, but it was waiting there within us nonetheless, needing
only a pinprick to flow out.
There was another thing, though, less altruistic and thus
maybe stronger. But for the grace of God, there through the

red mud trudged we, stoop-shouldered toward a brick-veneer house soon not to be our own. At three o'clock in the morning, once or twice or often, many of us had known ourselves to be potentially that small pale man as we sweated against the menaces of debt not to be covered by non-farm earnings or a job in town, of drouth, of a failing cattle or grain or peanut market, of having overextended ourselves on treasured land or machinery or a house, of perhaps a wife's paralyzed disillusionment with the rigors of country life, and above all of the onslaught of sickness with its flat prohibition of the steady work and attention that a one-man operation has to have, or else go under. The Loser had made us view the fragility of all we had been working toward, had opened our ears to the hollow low-pitched mirth of the land against mere human effort.

No, I didn't get the little A.-C. combine. If all of us there had been amateur buyers I would have had it for a hundred and seventy-five dollars, for that was where the other countrymen stopped bidding. But a dealer type in lizard boots and a spotless down jacket and a large black hat stayed with me, as I had suspected he would, for the old machine with a bit of furbishing would be worth seven hundred or so on his lot. Enjoying the growth of his cold resentment, I carried him up to four hundred and quit, partly because of my doubts about bulling that orange hulk through ninety difficult miles and perhaps getting caught by darkness, but mainly I believe because thinking about the Loser and all he stood for had made me start wondering hard if I really, honestly, badly needed the damned thing.

Nor did I stay to watch the bidding for the cattle and the house and land. What I wanted, and what I did, was to flee back home to black dirt and limestone country, where I could have a drink beside a fire of liveoak logs and consider the Loser's alien, sandy-land troubles with equanimity from afar.

John Graves (1920–2013) grew up in Fort Worth, graduated from Rice University, and received his M.A. in English from Columbia University. During World War II as a marine, he saw action in the Pacific and was wounded at Saipan. He taught briefly at the University of Texas in Austin, leaving to become a freelance writer, traveling to exotic places—Majorca and Tenerife, Spain; New York City; and New Mexico.

In the late 1950s Graves returned to Texas, taught for a time at Texas Christian University, and purchased Hard Scrabble, the four hundred acres in Somervell County near Glen Rose where he has worked both as a farmer and a writer ever since. His stories and articles have appeared in such venues as *The New Yorker*, *Town and Country*, *The Atlantic*, *Holiday*, *American Heritage*, and *Esquire*.

His best known work, *Goodbye to a River*, a personal and historical book based on an autumn canoe trip down a part of the Brazos about to be radically altered, was published by Knopf in 1960 and has been in print ever since. In 1973 Knopf brought out *Hard Scrabble* (now available from University of Texas Press), a collection of personal essays.

Graves was a past president, senior member, and fellow of the Texas Institute of Letters, which honored him with the Carr P. Collins Award for both *Goodbye to a River* and *Hard Scrabble*.

CPSIA information can be obtained
at www.ICGtesting.com
Printed in the USA
LVHW051331260523
748098LV00004B/25